Teaching Media
in Primary Schools

Education at SAGE

SAGE is a leading international publisher of journals, books, and electronic media for academic, educational, and professional markets.

Our education publishing includes:

- accessible and comprehensive texts for aspiring education professionals and practitioners looking to further their careers through continuing professional development

- inspirational advice and guidance for the classroom

- authoritative state of the art reference from the leading authors in the field

Find out more at: **www.sagepub.co.uk/education**

Teaching Media
in Primary Schools

edited by **Cary Bazalgette**

Los Angeles | London | New Delhi
Singapore | Washington DC

First published 2010

SAGE Publications Ltd
1 Oliver's Yard
55 City Road
London EC1Y 1SP

SAGE Publications Inc.
2455 Teller Road
Thousand Oaks, California 91320

SAGE Publications India Pvt Ltd
B 1/I 1 Mohan Cooperative Industrial Area
Mathura Road
New Delhi 110 044

SAGE Publications Asia-Pacific Pte Ltd
33 Pekin Street #02-01
Far East Square
Singapore 048763

Library of Congress Control Number: 2010921405

British Library Cataloguing in Publication data

A catalogue record for this book is available from the British Library
ISBN 978-1-84920-575-7
ISBN 978-1-84920-576-4 (pbk)

Typeset by C&M Digitals (P) Ltd, Chennai, India
Printed in Great Britain by MPG Books Group, Bodmin, Cornwall
Printed on paper from sustainable resources

In memory of James Learmonth
1939–2003

MEA is the subject association for everyone who teaches about the media at any level of the education system, including mainstream primary and secondary schooling, specialist media courses in the 14–19 phase, in informal education, and in teacher training and academic research. We also welcome media professionals with an interest in the development of media literacy.

Membership of MEA is free. By registering on the website at www.mediaedassociation.org.uk you join an online community through which you can network with colleagues in the media education sector and use the site's 'social bookmarking' functions in order to find the best resources, ideas and research, and to contribute your own evaluations. You can also post your own materials – writing, classroom resources, video and audio – for evaluation by others. By defining your preferences (educational sector, professional role, specific media, etc) you can sign up to receive news and information tailored to your own needs and interests.

MEA runs an annual conference, offering opportunities for professional development, for joining in debate about current issues in media education and in the media, and for meeting other media educators. Our magazine, PoV, is available free online, with new issues appearing three times a year. We welcome new contributors.

MEA is based in England but is open to media educators from around the world. www.themea.org

Contents

Acknowledgements

Guy Merchant thanks Rob Hobson of Halfway Junior School and Roz Wells of Brunswick Primary School in Sheffield for allowing him to draw on their innovative work in writing Chapter 8.

About the Editor and Contributors

Editor

Cary Bazalgette worked at the British Film Institute from 1979 to 2007, having previously been a teacher of English and film-making in London secondary schools. She has written and edited a number of classroom resources for media education and has published and spoken widely on this topic in the UK and around the world. She is now Chair of the Media Education Association, a member of the European Commission's Media Literacy Experts' Group, and a Visiting Fellow at the Institute of Education, University of London.

Contributors

Shakuntala Banaji is a lecturer and researcher at the Institute of Education's Centre for the Study of Children, Youth and Media. She lectures in Internet Cultures, Film Theory and Audiences and previously taught in London secondary schools as an English and Media teacher. She is currently researching Creativity and Innovation in schools across Europe for the EU's Institute of Prospective Technological Studies. Her previous project, CivicWeb, funded by the EU, examined young people's on- and offline civic participation in seven countries. She has worked on a number of research projects in relation to children, media and education, ethnicity, gender and news reception, Hindi cinema, multicultural citizenship, the internet and youth civic participation.

Tim Brook taught in primary schools in Hertfordshire and East Anglia for many years – latterly as a deputy then head teacher. Always interested in creativity and cross-disciplinary working, he explored the educational benefits of computers from their introduction into primary schools during the early 1980s, becoming a freelance specialist teacher and trainer in 2001. He created the website www.magiclanternlearning.co.uk, and has worked with many schools across the Eastern region as well as currently being Creative Media Director at St Felix CEVC Middle School in Newmarket.

Angela Colvert is Senior Lecturer in English Education at Roehampton University and is currently engaged in PhD research into alternate reality games (ARGs) in education, at the Institute of Education. Her research is based upon the findings of two long-term research projects which she undertook whilst teaching in a large south London primary school. She is an active member of the UK Literacy Association (UKLA).

Geoff Dean has been encouraging learners of all ages to 'read', make and enjoy moving image texts for over 40 years as a teacher, school manager and local authority adviser in three local authorities. He still works regularly in classrooms and trains teachers about how to use a range of media at the many courses he conducts around the country. He is the author of six books, mostly dealing with English, literacy and more able pupils, and contributed articles to the National Literacy Strategy handbook. He serves on the National English Board and is a senior A Level examiner.

Liesbeth de Block is a lecturer in Media Culture and Communication at the Institute of Education, University of London, and a Research Officer in the Centre for the Study of Children, Youth and Media. Her research focuses on the role of media in young peoples' social interactions and learning about society, particularly in the context of migration. She was previously a teacher and teacher trainer.

Janet MacPhee is Project Director for Peterborough's city literacy campaign 'READ.WRITE.inspire'. Through this work, Janet has sought and developed opportunities for children and young people that link literacy with media activities. She has been successful in encouraging many local and national businesses to take an active part in supporting the activities in schools across Peterborough, and is working on a Comenius-funded joint literacy and film project with schools in the Republic of Ireland.

Jackie Marsh is Programme Director of the Sheffield University EdD programme. She also teaches on the MA in New Literacies and the MA in Early Childhood Education programmes. She has conducted a number of research projects exploring how creative and innovative teachers have responded to the challenges of the new media age, and she led Digital Beginnings, a national survey of 0- to 6-year-olds' use of popular culture, media and new technologies in the home and early years settings. She was President of UKLA, 2005–2007, and co-edits the *Journal of Early Childhood Literacy*.

Guy Merchant is a professor of literacy in education and coordinator of the Language and Literacy Research Group at Sheffield Hallam University. He is research convenor for the United Kingdom Literacy Association (UKLA) and a member of the association's Executive Committee and National Council. Guy contributed to the Qualifications and Curriculum Authority's (QCA) working group on multimodality and is a critical friend to UKLA's international project Critical Literacy. He is a founding editor of the *Journal of Early Childhood Literacy*, and a member of the Editorial Advisory Board of *Literacy*.

Becky Parry worked as a teacher and then as Education Manager at the Showroom cinema in Sheffield where she established a range of projects including the Showcomotion festival, www.showcomotion.org.uk, and set up Cube www.cubeweb.org.uk, a practical media production and journalism project for young people aged 14–19. Her PhD research concerns children's engagements with film in relation to literacy, and she is currently a researcher on an ESRC-funded project to explore media education and learning progression at the Centre for the Study of Children, Youth and Media at the Institute of Education, University of London.

Geraldine Walker has worked within the primary sector for over 20 years and now works at an independent cinema in Sheffield as Education and Outreach Manager. Geraldine has developed training sessions for teachers looking at how film can be used creatively in all areas of the curriculum, particularly focusing on developing writing and reading skills. She is currently devising Insets and activity days for teachers and students to enhance KS2 languages and is working with Yorkshire Film Archives on a pilot scheme aimed at training teachers to use archive film in the classroom.

Chris Whitney has taught in both secondary and primary schools in London and Berkshire. She then moved to Lincoln where she is now the Primary English subject leader for the Lincolnshire School Improvement Service. In 2005–6 she attended the BFI training scheme for lead practitioners as part of the Reframing Literacy programme. Over the past three years, Chris has led a team of literacy consultants and leading teachers exploring the role of the moving image in Lincolnshire schools and developing a range of strategies for working with media in the primary curriculum.

Introduction

Cary Bazalgette

For more than a century, most children in the 'developed' world have entered schooling with a repertoire of ideas, impressions, stories and information gained from the popular media. Newspapers, posters, comics, film, radio, television, computer games and the internet have all contributed to the early learning of successive generations. For most of that time, it has been regarded as the business of schools to do their best to, as it were, delete and overwrite that learning, substituting the 'proper' forms of knowledge to be found in traditional, respectable media, like books.

This is now beginning to change. Despite the enormous impact of the mass media on 20th-century life, it has taken until the dawn of the digital age and the 21st century for policy-makers to start admitting that children might need to learn about the media in school (DCSF, 2009; EC, 2009). Before this, they had stubbornly resisted the lobbying, advocacy, research findings and pockets of good practice that have been emerging from enthusiastic teachers, advisers and academics since the 1930s (Bolas, 2009). Marginal references to media did squeeze into curriculum documents in many countries during the later 20th century, but they were more likely to be found in curricula for older children. In the UK, optional accredited courses in Media Studies and Film Studies began to be offered from the 1970s onwards, but just for students in the 14–16 and 16–18 age groups. Although primary-age children are the most avid consumers of media such as television, the idea that learning about this and other media might form part of their curriculum has continued to seem outlandish until very recently.

Nevertheless, over the last 30 years, there has been a steady, if small-scale development of thinking and practice about teaching media in the primary school. Several of the contributors to this book have played key roles in that development; the others have more recently gained new perspectives through classroom practice and research. Our aim in this book is to convert those who are still doubtful about the value of media education for younger children, and to inform and inspire those who are already enthusiastic. This is not a handbook or an instruction manual. It is a book of ideas and insights for the adventurous professional.

What is 'teaching media' supposed to be for?

The terms 'media education' and 'media literacy' remain confusing and alarming to many people, and their purposes seem unclear. In fact, they have probably become more confusing as they have seeped into different areas of policy and been taken up by a diverse range of agencies. At one level, we can differentiate the two terms very easily: media education is obviously a process, while media literacy is, equally obviously, an outcome of that process. But confusions remain. While many media educators – at primary and other levels – have tended to value popular cultural forms and identify positive ways in which they contribute to children's learning, the prime motivation for promoting the idea of media literacy at policy level has been anxiety about the effects of the media, particularly on the young. The urge to protect vulnerable others from social and cultural changes that we do not fully understand ourselves is, of course, an age-old phenomenon. Blaming the media for causing behaviour that might more logically be related to poverty, the availability of drugs, alcohol or guns, or more simply to being young, is also a well-established pastime for the middle-aged. But protection and blame do not form a promising basis for effective teaching. Teaching approaches that simply set out to prevent children from doing things are fundamentally flawed unless the threat is consistent and obvious. It does not take long to teach children not to play with fire or run into the traffic! Trying to teach them that there are dangers in something they already use and enjoy is more complex.

Realising this, industry sectors such as broadcasting, advertising, internet service providers and mobile networks have all started to produce 'media literacy' materials for schools, premised on the notion that, while it may be a waste of time educationally – as well as poor business strategy – merely to instruct children in the dangers that may lurk in their products, it is a good idea to provide schools with 'behind the scenes' resources that explain how these products are made. These can indeed be interesting and useful, but many are rooted in the false assumption that simply learning how to do something will also automatically develop a critical consciousness in learners and ensure that they become more discriminating media users (Bazalgette et al., 2007). In the hands of experienced media teachers, this may well happen, but most teachers lack the necessary contextualising skills.

The picture is further confused by corporate hyperbole from the information and communication technologies (ICT) industries, particularly the hardware sectors who would have us believe that a carefree technological paradise is always lying just around the next corner. From this perspective, teaching media in the primary school is all about the acquisition of ICT skills, and an essential route to the production of new cohorts of eager young consumers, avid for the latest kit. Most of the rhetoric around media and children or youth is dominated by the word 'technology': it is the technology that will change everything, we are told. But technology by itself doesn't change anything: change only happens when people appropriate technologies to serve their interests (Winston, 1998). It tends to be conveniently forgotten by technological prophets that none of the really major changes in communications of recent years – the internet, email, Google, wikis, mobile phones, texting and social networking – were anticipated by the experts. Each of these innovations was driven by social practices and small entrepreneurs, not by some technological juggernaut rolling inexorably on. Learning about the media in primary school can obviously involve some technological skills, just as learning music can involve learning how to play an instrument, but in both cases much of the key learning, especially at the outset, is concerned with the development of cultural and critical understanding. Being able to make music – or media – is hugely important, but it's not an essential starting point.

Children are people

So when we consider teaching and learning about the media with children in the classroom, it behoves us to remember that they too are people, engaged in social and cultural activity, with their own histories of engagement with media in a continuum from drawn and photographed images, through written and audio-visual texts to interactive games and websites. The most useful starting point for any media teaching in the primary school – and one that is free of any technological skills or specialist knowledge – is to ask children what media they most enjoy. What are their favourite DVDs and why do they like them? Who plays computer games and which are their favourites – and why? What have they seen recently on TV? Conversations generated by questions like these, conducted non-judgementally and with encouragement for children to provide more extended accounts of what they like, what they don't like, and why, can demonstrate to children that their home culture is respected and is of interest, rather than being something to be discarded at the school gate. It is of course necessary to be sensitive to the fact that, although it is households with children that are the most likely to contain numerous media devices, many of them in children's bedrooms, some homes have very few possessions and what media equipment they have may be old or broken. Rules about media use may also differ markedly between cultures and in different social groups, so it cannot be assumed that all the children in the class are likely to have had similar media experiences. But it is better to work out a way of having classroom conversations about media use that include everybody, rather than not having such conversations because they might exclude someone. It will often emerge that children have an awareness of media phenomena without actually having experienced them, because peer group and playground talk have ensured that key information is widely shared: Chapter 1 explores this phenomenon.

What are 'the media' anyway?

Most children (like the rest of us) encounter an entity such as, for example, Harry Potter, across novels, games, websites and films, not to mention press coverage and merchandising. What the educational system tends to do with this cultural soup is to segregate one privileged area – books – and make it the business of literacy, while the rest are lumped together under the rubric of ICT or of 'multimodal texts'. The term 'multimodal text' has been eagerly adopted by the literacy industry as a way of continuing to marginalise any medium other than print and to continue disregarding children's real cultural practices. Bearne and Wolstencroft (2007) make a persuasive case for including multimodality as part of the business of literacy, reminding us that it is not new, but an important and interesting concept that encourages us to look at how different elements of any text interact. It can usefully be applied as a comparative measure, as in 'television is more multimodal than comics'. But the term 'multi-modal texts', when used to group together everything that is not pure print, is an unhelpful neologism that obscures many crucial differences between types of text. In practice, it is often simply elided with ICT, as in this advisory document (Wirral, 2006: 4):

> The renewal of the frameworks places ICT clearly at the heart of raising standards in literacy. In response to this, advice and resources for the production of multi-modal [sic] texts will be released.

From the point of view of planning an educational strategy, it might make better sense to look at the whole mass of media texts that children encounter every day and consider them, not in terms of the technologies that produced them (which tends to end up as Books vs The Rest) but in terms of the kinds of decoding and comprehension skills that are required in order to make sense of them. This might help us work out what we really need to teach children in order that they can be literate for the 21st century, rather than the 19th. Such a consideration might lead us to recognise that many of the so-called technologies that are so excitedly proclaimed as new domains of essential skills – websites, email, blogs, texts – are in fact largely, if not entirely, based on the written word. They may include pictures and complex layouts – but are no more image-rich and graphically complex than your average 19th century theatre poster.

On the other hand, there is a large area of communications that does not depend much – if at all – on the written word, and which is barely taught in schools: radio, film, television, video and games. What these media have in common is what makes them difficult to teach, at least in the kinds of classroom and curricula we have now: they are all time-based media. They all depend on duration as an essential part of their meaning. Four of them are visual, of course (Chapter 4 documents the history of suspicions that has characterised schools' attitudes to the visual), but all of them have to be consumed in fixed time frames, like music. Books likewise take time to read, of course, but that time is under the reader's control: it can take as long as you wish, or are able, to read a book.

A new way of thinking about texts?

Looking at the media in terms of how we consume media texts, and the skills we need to do that, could offer us just two broad but logical

Page-based texts	Time-based texts
– books – newspapers – print and poster advertising – web pages – graffiti – SMS messages – DVD and games menus	– films – television programmes – radio programmes – podcasts – games – recorded music – visits to virtual worlds

Figure i.1   A different way of categorising texts

divisions: into page-based texts on the one hand, and time-based texts on the other (see Figure i.1).

Our educational system is geared to page-based texts. 'Page' no longer refers just to paper: websites have pages too, and we still expect to be able to print them off if we need to. Pages can thus be copied and distributed easily – at least in the systems we have currently established. The essential feature of a page-based text is not the technology that carries it, but the fact that it is static: we can look at it for as long as we want. When we encounter a time-based text, on the other hand, we can only look at it for as long as it wants us to. The key creative agency behind a time-based text is not the sound recordist or the cinematographer: it is the editor. Editors work in the medium of time: sequencing and layering sound, visuals, voices, music and silence to create complex, highly multimodal texts that reward detailed analysis.

Of course, there are overlaps and crossovers between page-based and time-based texts. Web applications – especially social media – can include animated graphics and films, but I would suggest that we rarely look simultaneously at both the page-based and time-based elements of a website, whereas we do look simultaneously at a photograph and its caption. TV, games and many websites often also incorporate 'crawling' captions and other text, but the crawl usually mimics the pace and direction of normal reading. It may well be that in the longer term, the page-based/time-based distinction could become increasingly blurred, but I suggest that it will never disappear completely.

I am not proposing the page-based/time-based categorisation as an essential project for rethinking the whole of human culture! I merely suggest it as a prompt towards considering what it is we may want to teach when we teach about media in the primary school. It is important to shift the agenda away from technologically determined categories and away from thinking about media learning primarily in terms of ICT-related skills. Instead, we need to think about media in terms of their social and cultural roles, and about our activities with media as textual practices, not as the utilisation of tools. To talk about 'using media' in the classroom ought to be as strange as talking about 'using poetry' or sitting down at home to 'use a soap opera'. All of us – adults and children alike – read, watch, listen to, play with, consume and make media.

Starting where the children are

This is why many of the chapters in this book – especially Chapters 1, 2 and 5 – are grounded in observation of how children engage with media and what they enjoy. It is also why the first part of the book is entitled 'Cultural Learning'. This is a two-way process. Children's early media experiences are an important part of their introduction to our culture: the shared ways of thinking and telling that bind us together. But teachers will also learn from the children about what these cultural experiences have meant: what the children value, and what they are good at. A key principle here is that children's early media experiences have given them a more sophisticated capacity for understanding time-based texts than the education system's print-oriented agenda allows for. Several chapters emphasise how teachers' assumptions about what children can do and understand have to be revised when they embark on teaching media. This can in turn have a longer-term effect on pedagogy when teachers realise that their pupils are rather more astute and knowledgeable, and sometimes more articulate, than they had thought, simply because the school had not valued what these children were actually good at; Chapters 6 and 7 explore this phenomenon. Assumptions about what films or games are suitable for a certain age group may also turn out to be wildly off-beam. But just as schools have a responsibility to extend children's experience of literature or music, so they should see it as a responsibility to extend children's media experiences, offering them new challenges and unfamiliar texts, as well as valuing the media texts they already enjoy; Chapter 3 makes this case in relation to film.

A preoccupation with the possible dangers of unsuitable content or inappropriate contacts has distorted much of the debate about 'media literacy' and dominated some teachers' approach to the topic. But this is not to say that the development of critical and analytical skills is not an important part of learning about the media. The second part of this book is entitled 'Critical Learning': its chapters argue for parity and indeed overlap between the critical skills required for traditional literacy and those required for media analysis. What emerges here is the potential homogeneity of literacy learning. Skills such as narrative prediction, inference of character traits and generic recognition are necessary for comprehending texts in any medium, and children are likely to have acquired an awareness of these concepts – if not formally articulated – from their media experiences before they start school. At a minimum, schools can increase children's chances of embarking on literacy learning with confidence if teachers can help them refer to and reflect upon the ways in which time-based texts signal character, narrative structures and genre. But by also making a more deliberate effort to foster and make explicit the specific skills needed to under-stand and appreciate time-based texts – for example, recognising how framing or lighting have contributed to meaning – teachers can help children grow in confidence as overall communicators, understanding the kinds of creative choices that are open to the makers of any kind of text.

Another way of understanding these creative choices is of course for children to undertake media production activities themselves, which is why the third part of this book is entitled 'Creative Learning'. The temptation here is to embark on large-scale projects such as film-making with the whole class. Our emphasis is on enabling children to have informal, recursive opportunities for creative activities with media: ones that allow them to reflect on their first efforts and to try again; to get feedback from real audiences and to respond to it; to move to and fro between different media, such as filmed and written stories. Chapters 8 and 9 emphasise approaches to the production of time-based texts that maximise every child's involvement and can be embedded in everyday classroom practice. It is not essential for chil-dren's media work to be shown to parents and treated as something out of the ordinary. Media production skills develop like any others. Children need the time to identify what has not worked well and to think about how they might improve it next time: this means having repeated opportunities to make small media texts for limited circulation, rather than high-profile productions. But of course both teachers and children will eventually want their work to be seen by others. Putting children's work into the public domain is fraught with anxieties about risk – anxieties that in the UK have now reached uniquely hysterical levels. Chapters 8 and 9 offer sober and practical advice on how to address these risks proportionately.

Taking the first step

These cultural, critical and creative strands of learning are promoted by the Charter for Media Literacy, which is invoked by several of this book's contributors.[1] The three strands work most effectively when interwoven, and, as all the contributors to this book argue, they can be embedded into the mainstream curriculum, rather than being taught as a separate 'media' project or topic. In some schools, however, it can still be difficult to justify media teaching unless it is presented as a special project with a visible outcome. Sometimes such projects are never repeated, so that what teachers and pupils learn from them is lost and may be forgotten. But it can also happen that a teacher's or a school's first experience of media teaching, whatever form it takes, generates an unexpected amount of thought and reflection that leads to the development of quite new approaches: it can have a catalytic effect on a whole school.

We are still at the early stages of defining our expectations about children's learning progression in media and in defining standards for assessment. Models for this have been devised before (Bazalgette, 1989; Film Education Working Group, 1999), but as classroom practice, research and the media themselves develop, new models will emerge. It already seems likely that using an 'ages and stages' model for children's progression in media learning may be unhelpful, and that children may be operating concepts such as 'authorial intent' in prototype form in their media learning, much earlier than traditional literacy learning frameworks have led us to expect.

This is why this book cannot provide a simple template for classroom activity. It is more like an invitation: we invite you to join a movement that will, we hope, not merely add another requirement to the curriculum, but transform our ideas about the very nature of literacy, and help us to offer children more pleasurable, purposeful and successful learning experiences.

Many people have contributed to the thinking and practice behind this book. However, I would particularly like to thank Terry Staples for his patience, his editorial advice and help, and for asking hard questions.

Note

1. See the Charter for Media Literacy at www.euromedialiteracy.eu (retrieved 3 January 2010).

References

Bazalgette, C. (ed.) (1989) *Primary Media Education: A Curriculum Statement*. London: British Film Institute.

Bazalgette, C., Harland, J. and James, C. (2007) *Lifeblood of Democracy? Learning about Broadcast News*. Available at www.ofcom.org.uk/advice/media_literacy/lifeblood/ (retrieved 31 December 2009).

Bearne, E. and Wolstencroft, H. (2007) *Visual Approaches to Teaching Writing: Multimodal Literacy 5–11*. London: Paul Chapman Publishing.

Bolas, T. (2009) *Screen Education: From Film Appreciation to Media Studies*. Bristol: Intellect.

Department for Children, Schools and Families (DCSF) (2009) *Children's Plan Two Years On: Next Steps to Achieve Outstanding Children's Services*. Press release, 14 December. Available at www.dcsf.gov.uk/pns/DisplayPN.cgi?pn_id=2009_0251 (retrieved 28 December 2009).

European Commission (EC) (2009) Press release, 20 August. Available at http://europa.eu/rapid/pressReleasesAction.do?reference=IP/09/1244&format=HTML&aged=0&language=EN&guiLanguage=en (retrieved 28 December 2009).

Film Education Working Group (1999) *Making Movies Matter*. London: British Film Institute (Appendix 2: 73–8). Also available at www.bfi.org.uk/education/research/advocacy/pdf/making-movies-matter.pdf (retrieved 3 January 2010).

Winston. B. (1998) *Media Technology and Society: A History – From the Telegraph to the Internet*. London: Routledge.

Wirral, Metropolitan Borough (2006) *Primary Literacy Subject Leaders' Update*. Available at www.wirral-mbc.gov.uk (retrieved 30 December 2009).

Part 1

Cultural Learning

Children's engagement with media is a cultural process. We need to understand what they know about media, what they can do and what they enjoy, before we decide how to help them build on and extend this cultural learning.

1

TV Talk and Children's Identities

Liesbeth de Block

Chapter objectives

This chapter focuses on the importance of talk about television in facilitating children's social relationships, especially across linguistic and cultural boundaries; in helping children to build their own identities and memories; and in helping social groups to bond together. The chapter also looks specifically at the role of talk about TV news programmes in the lives of migrant children and their families.

I first became interested in the role of media in children's social negotiations and relationships when I was working as a language support teacher with refugee children in a London primary school. I began to notice how often references to TV dominated the children's social interactions, games and jokes. My particular interest was in the ways in which 'TV talk' appeared to facilitate cross-cultural and cross-language relationships (de Block, 2002; de Block and Buckingham, 2007). Of course, other communication technologies are now increasing features of these playful interactions, but TV was dominant at the time of the research I will be discussing, and it remains children's favourite medium, so it will be my main reference point (Livingstone and Bovill, 2001).

Teaching and then becoming a researcher in the same school gave me unusual and privileged opportunities to observe a variety of children in different contexts, focusing on two groups in particular, one of boys (aged 10/11) and one of girls (8/9).[1] I spent 18 months 'hanging out' and observing in the playground; going out with small groups in the local neighbourhood and across London; visiting homes; working with children in the classrooms; and making videos. In this way, I was able to cross-reference and verify my conclusions and compare them with other research in related areas of childhood and media studies (Gillespie, 1995).

How does talk about television relate to questions of identity and belonging? Why is it important to study an area of social interaction that appears to be ephemeral and essentially transient? What is relevant in this for schools and teaching? In this chapter, I will offer a glimpse of some of the dynamics of TV talk so that you can build your own picture of how the children in your school use media, and consider what implications this might have for teaching, learning and school practice.

What is TV talk?

TV talk can take many different forms: chat, storytelling, a single word or phrase; non-verbal interaction in the form of games, gestures, role play; knowledge about producers and channels, the latest developments in technology and production methods, upcoming shows, etc. TV talk is an activity that has its own social rules, creating within the group a shared remembering, a bedrock on which friendships are formed and identities are played with. TV talk is collaborative, drawing on the group's shared experience; it evokes emotions, appeals to the affective and the humorous, and prompts that exploration of identity and belonging that is essential to the process of growing up and belonging to a particular community.

Memory and shared meanings

Both within the family and with friends in and out of school, television plays a significant role in building autobiographical memories or histories. Television can help to locate children in time and place in almost the same way that family photos or stories do (Spence and

Holland, 1991). Often the children referred to programmes they used to watch when they were younger. This acted to reinforce a shared history. In the boys' group, the names of programmes such as *Powerpuff Girls* and *Rug Rats* were called out and ridiculed, even though they themselves had in fact often watched them.[2] The girls expressed almost hysterical excitement when they remembered programmes such as *The Tweenies* or *Rosie and Jim*. These shows performed the same function as their playground games – that of building a group memory they could draw on in times of tension. Many of the games had been played so often, and many of the television stories told so many times, that they formed a resource the children could draw on for security – to overcome arguments or simply to 'belong'.

Some of the refugee and migrant children mentioned programmes they used to watch before they came to this country. Rhaxma, originally from Somalia, still enjoyed watching an Italian programme she had seen as a toddler when living in Italy, even though she no longer understood Italian. It offered her a personal historical reference point. She had no photos from that time but television kept the memory alive. Several children from very different origins drew on the global popularity of *The Simpsons*, which had become a point of continuity in their lives. For example, the Somali children had watched it in Somalia, in Kenyan refugee camps, in transition, and now in their new country of settlement.

In fact, *The Simpsons,* closely followed by *Rug Rats*, was omnipresent in all the different forms of TV talk. These two shows provided word-play, jokes, dialogue, verbal mimicry and endless storylines to be learned and retold in detail. The children could act out some scenes and characters without the need for words. They related to familiar everyday scenes and used them for reference and comparison with their own family lives. Above all, the programmes were funny and therefore adaptable to a range of purposes and situations.

Group dynamics

TV talk has several different starting points. A child will name a programme, or an incident or personality from TV, and call it out to see if it will be taken up by the others – a kind of 'auctioneering'. It was noticeable how often new children or those on the edges of the friendship groups would do this. They would offer a selection of programmes for the group and then have to either suffer rejection or be accepted into the subsequent group chat. It was a tense process that I witnessed time and again. Set phrases were often used: 'Did you see the one where ...?' (a trope *Friends* also uses, titling episodes 'The one with ...').

But there were also openers occasioned by an external prompt provoking a memory that started the ball rolling. One girl made a link, then taken up by others, between a tuna sandwich and an incident in *Kenan and Kel*. Similarly, when for some reason I got annoyed with the boys' group, they all spontaneously started to hold their breath because it had sparked a group memory of an incident in another programme.

Yet on several outings with the boys' group, I got the impression that this was not entirely random: the children were actively looking for prompts. There were some well-known local characters and places in the area where they lived that they used as part of their common knowledge on home turf. Beyond this, on unfamiliar territory, they would seek out and try to anticipate the prompts that cemented them as a group. On one outing, walking along London's South Bank, the boys' group lit on a busker playing the clarinet. One of them, Jima, had been trying to get back into the group after a rejected film choice. Now he seized the opportunity to lead the talk onto a secure knowledge base. He began to retell an incident in *The Simpsons* that featured a saxophone player. It took him several attempts but with the help of the concrete reference (despite this being the wrong instrument), he succeeded.

Humour and play

Once a story was established within the group as one of *their* stories, then a single word, movement or phrase was enough to provoke a response. So the longer story got honed down to just its punch line, or a wordplay or a gesture. Understanding this key word or action established group membership.

On some occasions, misunderstandings were incorporated into the talk and became established, unwittingly adding a new layer of humour and subversion:

Jima: Hank gets cussed by this man. He goes to him, 'It's been so long since your mother's bath that she smells of cocaine gas.'

Here, Jima mistook the word 'propane' for 'cocaine' in an episode of *King of the Hill* – probably partly because he did not know the word propane. But it fitted into his understanding of the form and, in fact, the context of his life in King's Cross, London, where drug dealing and use was clearly visible on an everyday basis and the children knew all about it. Jima saw 'cocaine' as subversive and therefore worth a joke with his friends. It fitted into the sense of the joke, so he got away with it. The others responded appropriately and it was never clear whether they got both the intended joke and the unintended joke, or only the former.

Music – singing and dancing

Singing and dancing form a large part of TV talk. Every playtime, you could see children singing in groups; the new children learning from the well-established children, the younger learning from the older. Mention of different programmes inevitably prompted the singing of the theme songs by both boys and girls. For the girls' group, when I first started working with them, the theme of the *Powerpuff Girls* was *their* song. Its words held a special meaning for them.

The Powerpuff Girls

Fighting crime, trying to save the world

Here they come just in time, the Powerpuff Girls

Powerpuff!

The Powerpuff Girls theme © 1998–2010, Cartoon Network: A Time Warner Company

At first, they would play out this girl power in the playground with great excitement but as time went on, only Rhaxma held on to the song and the programme. The others moved as the top ten moved, but they would return to the theme of girl power in various ways in their discussions and, through that, return to the theme song and the programme. It became a joke that Rhaxma still held to it so firmly and they would sometimes indulge her.

Knowing the words of songs was very important. Those who knew them well gained extra status in the group. One boy, who had been a real outsider for much of his school life and the butt of fairly recent bullying, suddenly flowered in the last term by becoming a music and dance specialist. At the school-leaving party, he was the centre of attention, with children watching and copying his dance moves; from this he gained significant status.

Both the girls' and the boys' groups used songs and music to create a sense of togetherness. When there was friction in the group, it was often a song, started by one of them with the others joining in, that would smooth the waters. It calmed the group and, while it lasted, created a very cohesive atmosphere.

Fear, emotion and the news

Of course, TV talk also touches on pain, fear and trauma. Soaps, for example, are absorbing for children because they offer a view into an adult world (Buckingham, 1987), touching their own fears, and offering ways of considering family and relationship issues which are important for them. Yet while the soaps' formulaic construction makes them safe, for them to perform the functions of real life it is essential to pretend they are not constructed. Buckingham (1996) stresses the emotional resonance that makes soaps popular across cultures (Ang, 1985; Miller, 1992) and applies it to the ways in which soaps offer the opportunity for public displays of emotion or, for children, an arena for trying out emotions publicly.

Soap-related discussions involve issues of modality and 'reality', but news programmes have even more direct meanings and generate different kinds of fears. News is generally considered to be an adult genre, but it is also increasingly assumed to be relevant to children's learning for the purposes of citizenship and inclusion: an assumption which tends to disregard, or avoid, its affective aspects. Children are thus offered contradictory perspectives: an adult agenda which sees news as important and necessary, and a child protection agenda in which it is boring or upsetting. What do these perspectives add up to? The fact is that children do watch some news items, even if they do not choose to, as news broadcasts are often on when they are around. This raises two issues: firstly, how children react to and are affected by news; secondly, within the discourse of citizenship and political inclusion, the extent to which children consider news to be important for their own education and knowledge about the world.

Being familiar with the news can be seen as a sign of growing up, dealing with adult issues and entering the public sphere; emotional difficulties are part and parcel of this process. Local news, in particular, directly affects children's sense of safety and, especially for girls, restricts their geographical movements. But for children who see conflict and trauma not as faraway events but as part of their everyday realities, watching the news becomes a different experience (de Block, 2008). You see on the screen what you yourself have experienced or what people you know are currently experiencing. There is a widespread assumption that interpretations of the news are shared and consensual. But while mainstream 'Western' news will roughly offer an agreed menu and 'position', in an increasingly global news environment, many children have access to a range of different news sources. What they and their families watch could well be taking a radically different political, cultural or social position from the Western mainstream.

Many of the families and children I talked to had a strong sense that the national UK TV news did not provide enough news from their parts of the world. Many preferred CNN as being more international; or they selected broadcasts from their own regions where available. There was almost a sense in which receiving news from beyond the national borders within which they now lived was a necessary part of their identities as migrant (Gillespie, 1995). In addition, national and 'Western' news was often seen as presenting a point of view that maintained the present world order (Boyd-Barrett and Srebery-Mohammedi, 1997; *Journal of Ethnic and Migration Studies*, 2006). By seeking out other news channels, these families were looking for different analyses of news events and a more global perspective.

I was struck by how often groups of children would refer to the international news when talking to each other. The dinner hall was often a place where major news items were shared. Some of this research was conducted at the time of the Balkan wars and much of the news conversation in the dinner hall revolved around this. Veton, who had recently arrived in the UK from Kosovo, was clearly very preoccupied, looking tired and pale. He was up late most nights watching CNN with his father and other members of the Kosovan community in London. One dinner time, a group of his class were sitting together when another child came and joined them. She cut across all the previous conversation and started talking about the bombing which had started the previous day. The group rapidly joined in, especially Veton, who made a great effort to contribute.

All the children were interested. They made connections between what Veton was saying and the reports they had watched on television. He described talking to his grandparents on the phone and what they had told his family: many houses in their area had been burned down. They could hear shooting nearby. People had come to their house for shelter.

The group conversation moved on but Veton continued to talk to me. He started asking me for more details about the shooting down of a helicopter as he hadn't understood everything he had heard. His interpretation was that the Russians were to blame as they had been the only ones to support Milosević in refusing peace talks. At this point, Jima joined the table and immediately said he had been watching the news and he agreed with Veton in saying that the Russians and the Yugoslavs (i.e. Serbs) were to blame. He made a connection between what was happening at that time with renewed fighting between Eritrea and Ethiopia, and what had happened there in the past.

This was all sophisticated, well-informed talk with deeply personal connections. For Veton, it must have been very important to be able to talk with peers about what was happening, especially since there appeared to be no forum for him to talk elsewhere outside the home. It also allowed him to find connections with the experiences of other children and realise that he was not alone. It was the development of a simple and effective public space within which new and old identities and relationships were being negotiated.

I observed similar conversations in greater or lesser depth many times. Knowledge of news and world events appeared to have high status and was used a lot in the group power play. For example, in the following extract, Jima uses his knowledge to create an effective put-down of his friend:

Samuel: Nelson Mandela

Jima: Shut your mouth. Stop being sad

Estava: What? Nelson Mandela?

Samuel: That's my country's president

Jima: It isn't your country's!

Samuel: Yeah. That's where I come from

Jima: You come from Kenya. He's President of South Africa, you fool!

Conclusion

If television can operate as a shared intercultural space for children, this has four important implications for the school curriculum, for teacher training and for raising awareness generally.

Should TV talk be incorporated more into the curriculum?

The present tendency is often to go in the other direction. For example, a storyteller visiting the school was horrified by my research, adding that her work was valued by the schools she went to precisely because she aimed to counter the influence of television. I have also encountered teachers who have stopped children from talking about TV at class news time, saying 'That's not "real life"'. The evidence that TV talk is a potential shared space which can facilitate talk about difficult issues should counter such censorship. However, it could be counterproductive merely to hijack TV talk from children's informal interactions and give it formal space within the curriculum. That is not its role or its strength. I learned a lot from talking about TV with the children, and this learning informed my teaching practice and approach as well as my knowledge of the children. What is important is a recognition of the ways in which informal talk can influence formal learning.

Should schools offer opportunities for talking about the news?

While news was an important subject for TV talk, it hardly existed in the formal life of the school. Why should this be so at a time when citizenship is a core part of the school curriculum? The Head of my daughter's school provided one answer. Shortly after September 11 2001, I asked her how the school was addressing the news. Her reply surprised me but I discovered it was not unusual, especially in schools that do not contain a diverse cultural and religious mix. She said that news was not the business of the school and that she didn't want to upset the children. The best thing was to carry on as usual. The fact that the children were watching it and talking about it, that most people and institutions in the world were completely preoccupied by it, that the world was changed by it, appeared to be irrelevant to her. The school, in her eyes, should be a haven of seclusion and safety. My feeling was that she did not actually know how to address it and therefore chose not to. I am not implying that this approach is widespread but it may be more common where the majority of teachers come from predominantly mono-cultural backgrounds.

Could video production be an important way to complement TV talk?

The video production work I undertook with the children was an invaluable part of the research (de Block and Buckingham, 2007;

CHICAM, 2004). I have not dwelt on this aspect of the research at any length here: the major relevant point is that it offered another view on how children use media in narrative and discussion. However, there were also factors that had curricular implications. Video work allowed the children to express themselves and share their experiences in a way that promoted both literacy and citizenship skills (see also Part 3: Creative Learning). The level of their technological competence, after a remarkably short training session, confirmed the possibility of incorporating media production into the primary school curriculum (Bazalgette, 1989). In addition, my study confirmed the importance, in the media world of the 21st century, of developing children's audio-visual skills. At present, audio-visual literacy is still only on the margin of formal learning; it needs to be incorporated much more comprehensively.

What role can TV talk play in multicultural school communities?

Children living with two or more cultures are often seen as disadvantaged, but this research showed a different picture. While carrying out the fieldwork, I sometimes watched the playground from an upstairs window, and noted that during playtimes children moved across the space in mixed groups, forming and reforming in different combinations. This contrasted starkly with the picture at the end of the day. Then, groups of parents would wait for their children, each in their separate ethnic group, with little interaction between them. The children would emerge and leave the school thus segregated. In modern society, where economics, communication and everyday life require the ability to move across cultural and international boundaries, how are we supporting children to maintain and develop the skills they naturally display in the playground? This has implications for research, for the curriculum and for the training of teachers and support staff. Campbell (2000: 38) states: 'Having multiple cultural identities is a natural response to living in a culturally complex cultural environment, and developing the ability to adapt to different cultural contexts may be one of the key learning areas of the curriculum of the future.' In this context, media appear to offer a readily available resource for children to explore their different identities (de Block and Buckingham, 2007). Space needs to be made for the discussion of different reality interpretations if a commitment to media literacy as social practice is to acquire real meaning.

Notes

1. Girls' group:

   Juba (8): born in London of Ghanaian parents.
   Morwen (8): born in London of Welsh and Grenadian parents.
   Nyota (9): from the Democratic Republic of the Congo, an asylum seeker.
   Rhaxma (8): from Somalia, a refugee. Had previously lived in Italy.

   Boys' group:

   Estava and Denis (12, twins): from Portugal with father in Angola.
   Jima (11): from Ethiopia, an asylum seeker.
   Samuel (11): from Kenya, an asylum seeker.

2. TV references:

   Friends – Bright/Kauffman/Crane Productions, in association with Warner Bros, 1994–2004
   Kenan and Kel – Nickelodeon, 1996–2000
   King of the Hill – Fox, 1997–2009
   Powerpuff Girls – Cartoon Network, 1998–2001
   Rosie and Jim – Ragdoll Productions, 1990–2004
   Rug Rats – Nickolodeon, 1991–2004
   The Simpsons – Fox Broadcasting Company, from 1989
   The Tweenies – Tell-Tale Productions in association with the BBC, from 1999

References

Ang, I. (1985) *Watching Dallas*. London: Methuen.

Bazalgette, C. (ed.) (1989) *Primary Media Education: A Curriculum Statement*. London: British Film Institute.

de Block, L. (2002) *Television as a Shared Space in the Intercultural Lives of Primary Aged Children*. Unpublished doctoral dissertation, Institute of Education, University of London.

de Block, L. (2008) 'The place to be: making media with young refugees', in J. Hart (ed.) *Years of Conflict: Adolescence, Political Violence and Displacement*. Oxford: Berghahn.

de Block, L. and Buckingham, D. (2007) *Global Media, Global Children: Migration, Media and Childhood*. London: Palgrave.

Boyd-Barrett, O. and Srebery-Mohammedi, A. (eds) (1997) *Media in Global Context: A Reader*. London: Edward Arnold.

Buckingham, D. (1987) *Public Secrets: EastEnders and its Audience*. London: British Film Institute.

Buckingham, D. (1996) *Moving Images: Understanding Children's Emotional Responses to Television*. Manchester: Manchester University Press.

Campbell, A. (2000) 'Cultural identity as a cultural construct', *Intercultural Education*, 11 (1): 31–9.

CHICAM (2004) *Final Research Report. CHICAM: Children in Communication about Migration.* Available at www.chicam.org (retrieved 7 January 2010).

Gillespie, M. (1995) *Television, Ethnicity and Cultural Change.* London: Routledge.

Journal of Ethnic and Migration Studies (2006) *After September 11: TV News and Transnational Audiences,* special issue, 32 (6).

Livingstone, S. and Bovill, M. (eds) (2001) *Children and their Changing Media Environment.* Mahwah, NJ: Lawrence Erlbaum.

Miller, D. (1992) 'The young and the restless: a case of the local and the global in mass consumption', in R. Silverstone and E. Hirsch (eds) *Consuming Technologies: Media and Information in Domestic Spaces.* London: Routledge.

Spence, J. and Holland, P. (eds) (1991) *Family Snaps: The Meanings of Domestic Photography.* London: Virago.

Points for Practice

Reading Images 1

Cary Bazalgette

This could be a regular, enjoyable short exercise that could include consideration of any issues or ideas that are raised in discussion of an image. Think of it as a 20-minute 'limbering up' exercise rather than as a complete session in itself. It could lead on to other media work or to writing, drawing, performance, talk or to activities in other curriculum areas. You could encourage children to bring in their own images for a 'Reading Images' session.

Find an image that you think the children will enjoy looking at and discussing. It could be a photo that you have taken, or downloaded from the web. It might relate to other work you are doing. Do not have your own 'agenda' about what you want children to get from it. The aim is to exercise their observation, imagination and talking skills, not to get 'right answers'. You may end up with differences of opinion.

Project the image onto the classroom wall or interactive whiteboard and ask the class to look at it quietly for one minute. Then ask them to talk with their neighbour about anything particular they have noticed.

You could then use any or all of the following questions to start discussion. Do not work through them mechanically. The session should be driven by what the children have noticed and are interested in. Your role is to prompt thinking and reflection by asking supplementary questions such as 'how can you tell?', 'what made you think that?', 'what else can you see?' or 'why do you think the photographer chose to show that?' (or, 'not to show that').

1. What can you see?
2. How close (or far away) do you think the photographer is?
3. [if there are people in the picture] Do you think these people/this person knew they were being photographed?
4. Is there anything you like in this picture?
5. Is there anything you don't like?
6. Is there anything that puzzles you in this picture?

You may have opportunities to explore features of the image such as focus (e.g. if some of it is in focus and some is not), colour, angle (e.g. high or low) and framing (e.g. close-up, wide angle, long-shot). But the aim is not to get children to use technical terms – discussion of these features may emerge from your prompt questions, and you should let their responses drive the discussion.

2

Social Networking Practices in Homes and Schools

Jackie Marsh

Chapter objectives

This chapter describes some of the research that tells us about how young children use social networking services (SNS) and virtual worlds. Arguing that these media promote children's early acquisition of essential literacy skills, the chapter describes how 4- to 7-year-old children have been helped to use blogs, Twitter and visual images in the classroom to promote literacy learning.

Social networking in the home

Social networking services (SNS) have proliferated in the 21st century and are now enormously popular with teenagers and adults. Facebook, MySpace and Twitter all have millions of users across a wide variety of social groups. However, most of the research in this area has focused on young people or adults, while public debate about children and SNS is almost entirely preoccupied with danger and risk. We need to better understand what children are actually doing with SNS before we jump to conclusions about the effects of these media and whether schools should be doing anything about them.

There is extensive evidence that young children are immersed in a wide range of media-related practices in homes from an early age (Marsh et al., 2005; Rideout et al., 2003). In these practices, they engage with a variety of texts that are multimodal in nature (Bearne et al., 2007). This fosters understanding of the affordances of different modes; that is, what a particular mode of communication, such as writing, sounds, still or moving visual images, offers in terms of meaning-making, and how these modes can combine and interact in texts. The types of textual engagement in homes observed in studies conducted by the University of Sheffield include reading books, comics and environmental print; reading a wide range of texts on screen; watching films, television programmes and screened advertisements; writing names, words, phrases, lists and stories on paper; and multi-modal authoring using computers. Through these activities, children become familiar with a wide range of genres, and begin to understand how these work as texts. Children also develop valuable skills through this multimedia, multimodal textual engagement, such as the ability to make inferences about texts – an ability which can be transferred across media (Kendeou et al., 2008). The rich set of literacy skills and knowledge which children acquire in this process is not always recognised in early years settings and schools (Levy, 2009a, 2009b; Levy, and Marsh, in press).

At the end of the 20th century, children's engagement in media texts at home was conducted primarily alone or with family members and immediate friends, but the 21st century has seen increased opportunities for engaging in communication with unknown others through the use of online social networking sites. One example of this phenomenon is young children's increasing use of online virtual worlds.

Online virtual worlds are immersive 2-D or 3-D simulations of persistent space in which users adopt an avatar in order to represent themselves, and interact with others. They may or may not include game elements. It has been estimated that there are now over 200 virtual worlds, either operating or in development, which are aimed at children and young people under eighteen[1]. Worlds particularly popular with children aged eight and under currently include Webzinz, Neopets, Club Penguin and Barbie Girls. In a study of 5–11 year-olds' use of virtual worlds, it was found that of 175 children completing a survey, 52 per cent reported using virtual worlds on a regular basis (Marsh, in press, a). A range of literacy practices is involved in the use of these virtual worlds. Children engage in instant messaging using chat facilities and can also send each other postcards, and read in-world texts or instructions for games. Multimodal skills are developed as users navigate complex screens and integrate different modes when they read the various in-world texts. In addition, children in this study reported accessing other sites that related to the virtual worlds. For example, some children searched YouTube for Club Penguin machinima[2]. These were films created by children and young people for other children and young people; it was this peer-to-peer culture that was taken up enthusiastically by the young children in the Marsh study (in press, a).

A number of anxieties have been expressed about children's use of virtual worlds. Valentine and Holloway (2002) summarised the negative stance adopted by some commentators thus: 'In the eyes of the debunkers, the "virtual" (the false, the inauthentic, the new, the disembodied) threatens to invade or pollute "the real" (the genuine, the authentic, the traditional, the embodied)' (Valentine and Holloway, 2002: 304). However, the Sheffield study evidence suggests that this dichotomy is false: there is a large degree of overlap between young people's online and offline worlds. The children engaged in online play with their school friends and siblings as well as with unknown others. There is thus a continuum between play and communication in offline and online activities, with all these activities taking place in the 'real' world.

Other social networking activities occur in the context of young children's daily lives, such as the use of mobile phone text messaging, instant messaging services and chatrooms, with adults acting as scribes (Marsh et al., 2005). All of these encounters offer children a broad perspective on literacy, which emphasises its function as a social and cultural practice. It is, therefore, important for early years settings and schools to embed these uses of literacy into the curriculum in order to ensure continuity between home and school domains.

Social networking in early years settings and classrooms

There is a range of ways in which social networking sites can be used in classrooms to foster the development of literacy skills. One nursery used blogging in order to engage young children in digital literacy practices that integrated home and school experiences.

The blog was developed by children in the nursery of Sharrow School, Sheffield, which was subject to a new build in 2005–2006. The architects

Figure 2.1   Sharrow Nursery's blog

who designed the school were very forward looking and created a blog in which they informed the community about the progress of the re-build. To capture the imagination of the children, they featured two small teddy bears, named 'Brix' and 'Morta', who were used to report the news. Once the building was complete, a separate blog was set up titled 'The adventures of Brix and Morta'[3] (see Figure 2.1).

Brix and Morta were placed in a backpack, along with a digital camera and a letter to families. The backpack was then sent home with children for a week at a time. The letters asked families to help children to take photographs of Brix and Morta having adventures with the children. At the end of the week, children brought the backpack back to school. They sat with an adult as the photographs were uploaded to the blog. The children then talked about each photograph and what they said was scribed by an adult so that it could be typed in to the blog post. Each child uploaded about five photographs and related stories to the blog before it was someone else's turn. The blog thus became a record of Brix and Morta's adventures with a number of families.

The value of a blog is that it is openly accessible on the web, which meant that parents and other family members were able to read the blog and, in some cases, even comment on it. Four-year-old Zakariya, for example, was the first to contribute to the blog. His parents had lived in Sheffield for many years, but had relatives living in Bangladesh.

THURSDAY, 6 MARCH 2008

Adentures with Zakariya: Episode 5

Zakariya was feeling poorly and so Brix and Morta helped him feel better.

They made me better with the doctor toys. They listened to my heart.

POSTED BY JACKIE MARSH AT 02:53   9 COMMENTS

Figure 2.2   Zakariya's post

The parents were keen to be involved in the project and enjoyed having the teddies and camera at home for a week. On the teddies' return, Zakariya had lots of adventures to report (see Figure 2.2):

One of the affordances of blogs is that commentators can leave messages for bloggers, a facility used by overseas relatives. Figure 2.3 outlines an observation from Zakariya's uncle in Bangladesh:

Anonymous said...

i am happy to see zakaria work.i am zakaria uncle
Bangladesh

08 March 2008 01:42

Figure 2.3   Blog comment from Zakariya's uncle

This is an example of how blogging can be an excellent means of enabling families, in any location, to keep in touch with children's interests. It also provides a means of encouraging young children to engage in the kind of participatory practices that are commonplace in the digital age (Jenkins et al., 2006).

While blogging is probably the most widely adopted SNS used in schools, other utilities are being used. Marsh (in press, b) outlines the work of a teacher of six- and seven-year-olds in the north of England, Martin Waller. He allows the children in 'Orange Class' to use Twitter to log their thoughts and activities over the course of a school day. Twitter enables users to upload to the internet messages containing up to 140 characters, known as 'tweets'. Users can log accounts of their activities over the course of a day and can foster the kinds of identity play and performance seen in the use of other SNS (Dowdall, 2009; Ito et al., 2008). Martin also enables the children to upload their photographs on Twitpic, which are then attached to their 'tweets' and used to extend the children's communication, or reinforce their messages. Adults and other children use Twitter to respond to 'Orange Class'; in this way, Martin ensures the children have an external audience for their work. As Merchant (in press) suggests:

> This raises questions about what happens as bounded classrooms are connected to diverse and fluid networked spaces with new possibilities for presenting, exchanging and making meaning. Others studies (Burnett, 2009; Merchant, 2009) have suggested that teachers feel challenged once children move into fluid networked spaces and begin to explore their own paths.

Merchant refers here to a previous study of his in which teachers in a northern city in England were engaged in the creation of a virtual world for a specific group of primary schools. The teachers could not easily embrace the concept that the children were autonomous within the world, and placed restrictions on them, such as not allowing them to let their avatars fly (Merchant, 2009). But in working with SNS in the classroom, educators need to cede some of the power normally entrenched in their role as authority figures, and to allow the children to lead learning in some of these spaces. This does not mean that teachers should play a passive role; there is much to do in terms of facilitating learning in SNS. However, Merchant's work is a reminder of the challenges to be faced as we move into an era in which pedagogy and curricula have to move from being teacher-directed to learner-led.

Conclusion

This chapter has offered a brief overview of the role that social networking services have in children's home environments, and has identified ways in which schools have begun to use them to promote relevant literacy activities. If one examines children's engagement with media texts over the last decade, it is clear that their involvement in online communication is becoming highly significant. These practices are not only popular with older children and young people, but are becoming an important part of children's informal early learning. Therefore, there is a need to identify what young children are doing with SNS and how this is impacting on their literacy learning. It is also important that teachers and early years educators are aware of the SNS experiences that children are likely to have had before they start school, so that curricula and pedagogy can be built on these foundations. If schools are to offer educational experiences that are relevant for a new media age, then these practices are as important as the various other reading and writing activities in which children engage. As Jenkins et al. suggest:

> Literacy skills for the twenty-first century are skills that enable participation in the new communities emerging within a networked society. They enable students to exploit new simulation tools, information appliances, and social networks; they facilitate the exchange of information between diverse communities and the ability to move easily across different media platforms and social networks. (Jenkins et al., 2006: 55)

Children in the earliest stages of formal schooling should not be left out of the move to a digital, participatory media culture, and it is possible to create pedagogical and curricular opportunities which rise to this challenge.

Notes

1. From KZero research, reported in December 2009 at www.kzero.co.uk (retrieved 2 January 2010).
2. A term which conflates 'machine' and 'cinema' – these are films created in computer games and virtual worlds using screen-capture software.
3. See http://brixandmorta.blogspot.com

References and Further Reading

Bearne, E., Clark, C., Johnson, A., Manford, P., Mottram, M. and Wolstencroft, H. (2007) *Reading on Screen*. Leicester: United Kingdom Literacy Association (UKLA).
Burnett, C. (2009) 'Research into literacy and technology in primary classrooms: an exploration of understandings generated by recent studies', *Journal of Research in Reading*, 32 (1): 22–37.

Dowdall, C. (2009) 'The texts of me and the texts of us: improvisation and polished performance in social networking sites', in R. Willett, M. Robinson and J. Marsh (eds), *Play, Creativities and Digital Cultures*. New York: Routledge.

Ito, M., Horst, H.A., Bittanti, M., Boyd, D., Herr-Stephenson, B., Lange, P.G., Pascoe, C.J. and Robinson, L. (with Baumer, S., Cody, R., Mahendran, D., Martínez, K., Perkel, D., Sims, C. and Tripp, L.) (2008) *Living and Learning with New Media: Summary of Findings from the Digital Youth Project*. The John D. and Catherine T. MacArthur Foundation Reports on Digital Media and Learning. Available at http://digitalyouth.ischool.berkeley.edu/report (retrieved May 2009).

Jenkins, H., Clinton, K., Purushotma, R., Robison, A. and Weigel, M. (2006) *Confronting the Challenges of Participatory Culture: Media Education for the 21st Century*. An occasional paper on digital media and learning, the John D. and Catherine T. MacArthur Foundation. Available at http://digitallearning.macfound.org/site/c.enJLKQNlFiG/b.2108773/apps/nl/content2.asp?content_id={CD911571-0240-4714-A93B-1-D0C07C7B6C1}andnotoc=1 (retrieved May 2009).

Kendeou, P., Bohn-Gettler, C. White, M.J. and van den Broek, P. (2008) 'Children's inference generation across different media', *Journal of Research in Reading*, 31 (3): 259–72.

Levy, R. (2009a) '"You have to understand words ... but not read them": young children becoming readers in a digital age', *Journal of Research in Reading*, 32 (1): 75–91.

Levy, R. (2009b) 'Children's perceptions of reading and the use of reading scheme texts', *Cambridge Journal of Education*, 39 (3): 361–77.

Levy, R. and Marsh, J. (in press) 'Literacy and ICT in the early years', in D. Lapp and D. Fisher (eds) *Handbook of Research on Teaching the English Language Arts* (3rd edn). London: IRA/ NCTE: Routledge.

Marsh, J. (in press, a) 'Young children's play in online virtual worlds', *Journal of Early Childhood Research*.

Marsh, J. (in press, b) 'The ghosts of reading past, present and future: material resources for reading in homes and schools', in K. Hall, U. Goswami, C. Harrison, S. Ellis and J. Soler (eds) *Interdisciplinary Perspectives on Learning to Read: Culture, Cognition and Pedagogy*. London: Routledge.

Marsh, J., Brooks, G., Hughes, J., Ritchie, L., and Roberts, S. (2005) *Digital Beginnings: Young Children's Use of Popular Culture, Media and New Technologies*. Sheffield: University of Sheffield. Available at www.digitalbeginnings.shef.ac.uk (retrieved January 2009).

Merchant, G. (in press) 'Web 2.0, new literacies, and the idea of learning through participation', *English Teaching: Practice and Critique*.

Merchant, G. (2009) 'Literacy in virtual worlds', *Journal of Research in Reading*, 32 (1): 38–56.

Rideout, V.J., Vandewater, E.A. and Wartella, E.A. (2003) *Zero to Six: Electronic Media in the Lives of Infants, Toddlers and Preschoolers*. Washington, DC: Kaiser Foundation.

Valentine, G. and Holloway, S. (2002) 'Cyberkids? Exploring children's identities and social networks in on-line and offline worlds', *Annals of the Association of American Geographers*, 92 (2): 302–19.

Every Picture Tells a Story 1

Geraldine Walker

This is a simple exercise in alerting children to the expressive possibilities of still images, encouraging reflection on what they can tell and show in a drawing, and sharpening their awareness of audience response.

Give pupils three squares and ask them to tell a story in three pictures with a beginning, middle and end.

They are not to tell anyone what the story is about and there is to be no writing involved. They then give their story to a partner who has to read the images, and tell the story back to the creator. The reader cannot be contradicted – their version is as they see it and is true as they see it. The other partner then has their turn.

If children are not confident with drawing, they can be encouraged to use stick figures. If they wish, they can draw people or animals or they could use basic shapes to tell a story.

Developments

1. The story can then be written underneath and if the pupil has English as a second language, they can write two versions, or write in their own language and tell the story in English.
2. They decide which story they would like to develop or, if possible, combine the two and then develop their ideas into a larger story – perhaps based on six or nine squares – depending on the age and ability of the children.
3. The pupils can be asked to draw the beginning of a story, pass it on to another who draws the next parts; this then passes on to a third party to finish off the story, so there are nine squares in all. The group can then discuss the story and decide how to tell the story to the class or develop it as a drama/narration or in written form.
4. Use images from magazines and newspapers instead of drawings.

Extending Children's Experience of Film

Cary Bazalgette

Chapter objectives

This chapter describes children's consumption of mainstream films and argues that, through their extensive pre-school experience of films, children starting school are ready to watch more challenging film material and can engage with films at a more sophisticated level than they can with print.

What is the point of teaching about film in the primary classroom? For most teachers, film is an acceptable stimulus for writing or talk, or an entertainment for after school or end of term, but the idea of seeking to enhance and develop children's expectations and critical skills specifically in relation to film tends to generate more ambivalent reactions.

Children's film consumption

This reflects the ambivalent cultural status of film in the UK. Mainstream Hollywood massively dominates our film distribution system, nowhere more so than in the children's and family film market. High production values in the form of lavish special effects, stunning animation and well-crafted scripting ensure a constant flow of films that adults and children can enjoy together. Many of the verbal gags and most of the esoteric cultural references go over the children's heads, but easily recognisable characters, predictable themes and amazing action sequences can quickly recapture their attention. The speed and technical complexity of these films ensures a thriving DVD market, with children collecting their favourites and watching some sequences repeatedly. As Disney realised back in the 1940s, films that appeal to children have a long shelf life, especially if they are animated and have fantasy or adventure settings that do not date.

For most parents, this wealth of Hollywood product is a godsend. In an increasingly risk-averse culture, it keeps children safely entertained; for the many families where both parents have to work long hours and/or have cramped living conditions, it buys a bit of time in a stressful schedule. For teachers however, it simply reinforces the perception that film is nothing to do with school. These mainstream products essentially *are* film as far as teachers are concerned, and therefore there is no need for school to pay any further attention to them or to be particularly discriminating in their use.

Teachers, like most other adults, have graduated from Hollywood product for children and moved on to mainstream movies for adults. Market statistics on film consumption tell us that a predominantly female group such as primary school teachers is likely to stick to mainstream genres such as romance, melodrama, musicals, comedy and historical drama rather than action, thrillers and sci-fi when they go to the cinema or borrow a DVD (UK Film Council, 2009, Chapter 15). As in the population at large, primary teachers who seek out non-mainstream English language films, let alone foreign language films, are in a minority. Film is assumed to be for entertainment and relaxation: the idea that it could be taken seriously, or even studied, is often seen as weird or nerdy. All the while, the press continue to mock Media Studies and Film Studies as options for older students, and the idea filters down to primary teachers and to parents that watching films in the classroom must be a suspect, time-wasting activity.

Cultural sources of mainstream films

In this context, the fact that children's film consumption comes almost entirely from a single, foreign source seems irrelevant. Most people accept that films – 'proper', successful films, anyway – just *are* American. If children enjoy a film, why should we care if it is American? And, in any case, surely 'American' doesn't really count as 'foreign'? The alternative would be films with subtitles, which few adults expect children to be willing to bother with.

Some will assert that, although UK children's film consumption is dominated by US products, at least the TV programmes they watch are mainly created in the UK, particularly by the BBC. Parents and teachers who grew up in the last two or three decades of the 20th century tend to retain an affection for the Children's BBC of their childhood and to regard it as one of life's certainties. Unfortunately, increasing economic pressures affect television as much as any other business and the first decade of the 21st century has seen a steady cutback in the amount of money spent by all TV companies, including the BBC, on original indigenous production for children. The most expensive programmes – live drama and documentary – have suffered most; the favoured alternative is to import programmes, particularly animation, and particularly from the USA. So now the overall tendency in UK children's entire audio-visual culture – not just their film viewing – is for it to be dominated by material from the USA.

Another way of looking at this is to see it as a very successful example of cultural imperialism. For nearly a century, the USA has recognised the importance of cinema in its global role (Nowell-Smith and Ricci, 1998). This role may be interpreted as 'spreading freedom and democracy' or as 'dominating world markets' – or both – but either way, films are a successful way of establishing American culture as both 'normal' and 'desirable'. However benign it may seem, and however delightful many of the films may be, the domination of children's culture by US-originated product remains a significant factor in ensuring the UK consumer's 'brand loyalty' to the USA.

To add this issue to the ever-growing catalogue of responsibilities lobbed by government into schools could seem excessive. There is in any case a default position, adopted by generations of education policy-makers, that the school has to function as a counter-balance to the assumed crassness and mediocrity of commercial audio-visual culture. Media prominence is given to hearsay accounts or dubious research that claim to prove a malign influence on children's mental and physical development from being 'parked' in front of television or DVDs (as though toddlers were readily amenable to 'parking'). The purpose of literacy teaching is popularly supposed to be that it weans children off films and TV and on to books. Time spent watching moving images is time wasted, it is assumed; or worse still, it is time 'taken away' from proper literacy learning and therefore must be contributing to lack of attainment.

What do children learn from watching films and TV?

However, instead of falling back on culturally determined prejudices about moving image media and their unproven ill effects, we could try working with the hypothesis that, if films and TV programmes are considered as 'texts', then children's encounters with these media could be regarded as textual experiences, through which they might be learning about how these texts function, over and above anything they are absorbing in terms of content. We need to bear in mind that moving image media play a large role in almost all children's early textual experiences, even in book-rich households. By the age of six months, most babies are spending some time in front of a television; by the age of two, the majority of children know how to turn the TV on by themselves. By five, almost all children can choose and load a DVD into a player or computer, and make selections from a menu. Contrary to the popular myth that children are abandoning TV for other, newer media, 64 per cent of five- to seven-year-olds say that TV is the medium they would miss most if it was taken away, and by age 11, children are still watching an average of 16.5 hours of TV every week (Ofcom, 2008).

Given the acknowledgment that, in becoming literate, children do not just learn to read, but also become familiar with books as a medium, it may be pertinent to consider what they may have learned from their early viewing about film and TV as media. It is of course virtually impossible to research what very young children make of these media, but close observation of babies and toddlers watching TV can generate some interesting hypotheses. For example, babies confronted with a zoom-in to a close-up of a face may lean away or pull their heads back: we may hypothesise that they have not yet learned the convention of a zoom, so it may just seem to them that a face is suddenly getting uncomfortably close. Older children can easily understand common-place devices such as a cut from a long-shot to a close-up: very young children may not recognise that the second shot shows bigger or more detailed parts of what was also there in the first.

We can be sure that by the time they are approaching school age, children understand conventions like these, because if they didn't, they wouldn't be able to enjoy films and TV as much as they do. We also know that they must have *learned* these conventions: they are not all 'natural' and self-evident, although some film conventions do replicate the way we perceive and interpret things in the real world. For example, when we see a character look off-screen, we expect the next shot to show us what they are looking at. This mimics an instinctive human reaction (Messaris, 1994). But other conventions are artificial. For example, a sequence of three shots, showing someone getting into a car, then entering a building, then sitting down in a room, expects us to take the omitted actions for granted. The first use of 'jump cuts' like this startled and confused audiences in the early days of cinema, as did the first close-ups (Gish, 1969).

Toddlers learn these conventions easily, by themselves, at the same time as they are learning the much more complex grammar, vocabulary and usage patterns of verbal language. But we could value and analyse their acquisition of filmic language, even if it has been gained easily. As well as close-ups and jump cuts, children learn the significance of different kinds of transition between shots: for example, where a slow fade or a leisurely dissolve signifies the passing of time. They learn that some sounds 'belong' in the world of the film: what characters say, noises made by objects they can see, like guns or trains, or even things they can't see, like birdsong or church bells; and they also learn that some sounds – especially music – do not literally 'belong' in the world of the film, but are conventionally put there to heighten the meaning: exciting action, for example, or impending danger. They learn to interpret a fast sequence of shots that alternate between, say, someone running and someone else clinging to a cliff edge: they realise that these are actions taking place at the same time.

The value of children's early experiences with film and TV

It would be easy to dismiss these observations. There is a pervasive view that films merely 'show' us things; that they are not really constructed, like real art. But in fact it is film's very success as a popular medium that tends to blind us to the richness and subtlety of its meaning-making processes. Anyone who has the opportunity to sit down and analyse even a simple sequence of moving images and sounds, or has had a go at editing some elements of sound and image into a coherent statement, is transformed by the experience. Film-makers aspire to represent the physical and emotional experiences of being in the world. Their creative choices, after story, setting and action, include framing, colour, lighting, movement, juxtaposition, sequence, voice, music, sounds, silence, transitions and duration, all of which affect each other in the meaning-making process. Film is, in other words, highly multimodal: its meanings are created through the interplay of these modes.

But what is important about the child's first encounters with this complex medium is not the extent to which they do or do not appreciate this multimodality. It is – as in their first encounters with any human endeavour – that they start to recognise the role of people in making meaning. Communication and expression are social activities. Playing games, speaking, singing, listening to voices, music and sounds, reading, writing, drawing, watching film and TV all offer us ways to enter the social world and to start seeing ourselves as participants. Children start school with a repertoire of skills, aptitudes and aspirations, drawn from the full range of communicative experiences available to them from babyhood onwards. Moving image media are an important part of that range, and make a significant contribution to children's emergent literacy.

As well as starting to understand the meaning-making techniques and devices specific to moving image media, children also gain generic comprehension skills from their film and TV watching. The fact that narratives have a structure, and that you can often make inferences about what kind of structure a particular narrative is likely to have, is one of the things that we need to know in order to anticipate the pleasures of reading or writing a story. This knowledge is established and reinforced by the moving image narratives that children learn to follow from their early years of film and TV viewing, whether or not they are also learning it from having stories told or read to them. The fact that many stories fit into generic categories is likewise supported by the experience of watching and enjoying moving image media. Films and TV offer practice in identifying character types, not only from what characters say but also from how they look and move. Spotting key features of a setting that provide clues about where and when the story takes place, or what may be going to happen, is another pleasurable aspect of film and TV viewing that later translates into realising the importance of descriptive passages in written and spoken stories.

To recognise this early learning flies in the face of 'commonsense' assumptions about the role of moving image media in children's early development. But commonsense is often fed by common misconceptions and prejudices. A sector of polemical publishing that makes selective use of medical and psychological research thrives on stoking up public anxieties about television watching and other media activities by young children (Sigman 2005, Palmer 2006). Educational research and classroom experiences offer a different perspective: the fact is that children are arriving in school with substantial media experience, and whether or not we believe that this is desirable, we can still derive positive outcomes from it. Teachers who acknowledge and seek to build on children's film-related literacy skills consistently report overall gains in attainment (Marsh and Bearne, 2007) and research in the USA into the role of early narrative understanding in predicting future reading comprehension indicated a link between TV-watching 'expertise' in six-year-olds and higher levels of reading attainment later on (van den Broek, 2001).

Three challenges

However, to acknowledge the relationship between film viewing and traditional literacy skills is only part of the story. It simply takes us back to the already accepted strategy of showing films in order to stimulate writing. Clearly this works, but it still sells children short. We also have to acknowledge that in becoming expert viewers of film and TV in their early years, children have developed film-related skills in inference, prediction, character type identification and genre recognition that can be well ahead of their ability to deploy these skills as readers. This insight presents us with three challenges:

1. Managing different levels of complexity in films and books

Children in their first years of schooling are already seeing films that are more complex and sophisticated than the books they are being offered as beginning readers. At five years old, many children clearly do not understand some of what is going on in, say, *Up* (dir. Docter and Peterson, USA, 2009), but nevertheless it asks them to engage with multiple time frames, playful shifts between realism and fantasy, unexpected twists and turns in the exposition of character, and

Figure 3.1   Three-year-old Kazi enjoys watching her favourite film (the Czech animation *Krteček* by Zdeněk Miler) and having a good cry

conflicting moral imperatives. Children will also watch the film in the context of a cinema audience or a family group, experiencing it as a collectively consumed text whose 'boring' or 'difficult' bits are nevertheless enjoyed by older children and adults. Thus the very experience of watching the film is potentially aspirational: it encourages children to want to watch it again. It is foolish to view this negatively and to see traditional literacy teaching as a struggle to compete with another medium. It is better to acknowledge and build upon the literacy skills that children have already acquired from their film viewing, by regularly undertaking some critical analysis of film in the classroom (see 'Talking about a Film', page 85).

2. Extending the cultural range of children's viewing experiences

A group of children in Peterborough who had seen a film about Kurdish refugees in Amsterdam, *The Boy Who Stopped Talking* (dir. Sombogaart, Netherlands, 1996), were keen to explain to me why they liked it so much. One girl said 'You know what, Miss? We're sick of magic!' The film had made them realise that their experience of realistic, live action drama dealing with strong themes related to their own lives (Peterborough has a huge migrant population) was extremely limited; they were eager to see more.

Children may be able to understand and enjoy richer, more complex and thematically 'difficult' films than those they usually encounter. It is a corollary of the family film's commercial success that children go on seeing much of the same kind of mainstream entertainment films for most of their childhood. They may get more from them as they get older and learn to enjoy the wisecracking and the irony, but they are still seeing a relatively narrow generic range from what is effectively a single cultural source. This is not – or should not be – a situation we would accept in relation to poetry, stories, music or art. There is therefore no good argument for ignoring it in relation to a medium that children already know well and enjoy.

There are some practical reasons for the narrow range of films available to UK children. The dominance of Anglophone films for children in mainstream cinema means that distributors shrink from the risks involved in trying to launch children's films from other cultures. As a result, most UK children are ignorant of such films. They are less familiar with subtitles than, say, Dutch or Danish children: their teachers and parents subscribe to the usually untested prejudice that children cannot cope, or wouldn't want to try and cope, with reading subtitles – forgetting perhaps that, in their familiarity with computer games and websites, their children are probably more used than they are to reading titles at the bottom of a screen. So children absorb the folk wisdom that subtitles are something to be avoided. But in 25 years of watching subtitled films with children, I have never seen any child get fed up with a good film merely because it had subtitles.

Teachers can play a key role in developing the quality of children's engagement with film, but deciding what films to use can be tricky. Showing short clips can be useful for specific and limited purposes such as exploring a particular technique, but it is always frustrating for children and an injustice to the film-maker if the children do not get to see the whole film as well. One answer is to focus classroom work on complete short films, which tend to offer a wider range of stylistic forms and are often dialogue-free, conveying their stories purely through filmic language (see 'Finding Films to Watch', page 46.)

3. Are children being unnecessarily failed?

Some children who are struggling with reading and writing may be able to succeed at interpreting, analysing and even making moving image texts. Many teachers, when working with film, have had their expectations about particular children's abilities confounded. Children who 'never write' have discovered new confidence and written great screeds when engaging with a medium with which they feel confident. Children who rarely contribute to discussion become articulate when discussing a film. Children whose concentration is minimal are suddenly absorbed for hours when faced with the challenge of editing a sequence of moving images.

It is thus essential to raise your expectations about what kinds of film children may be able to understand, and to recognise that children may be able to access, through films, concepts that they may not be able to access through written texts. Again, this requires sensitivity to children's own responses and readiness to consider interpretations that you had not thought of. Analysis of film does not have to be confined to discussion and written work. One of the benefits of digital technology is the opportunities it can afford for experimental work: small-scale exercises rather than full-scale film-making (see Chapter 9).

Conclusion

The point of teaching about film in the primary classroom is that, first and foremost, the ability to enjoy and analyse film needs to be seen as an integral part of literacy, not as an extra or a stimulus. As developing, critical and creative beings, children are entitled to have their film knowledge recognised, enhanced and extended. Teaching about film alongside other textual forms helps children to understand the place of print literacy within the wider world of communications, and to understand the nature of different kinds of text. Understanding how moving image media communicate through multiple, interacting modes, can ensure that as children get older, they can bring critical skills to the interpretation of news, advertising and other persuasive or informational texts. Furthermore, it should open their eyes to the possibilities of moving image media, encouraging high expectations of what film and TV can achieve in helping us to understand the world.

References

BFI (2008) *Reframing Literacy*. Available at www.bfi.org.uk/education/research/teach-learn/pdf/reframing_literacy.pdf (retrieved 28 December 2009).

Gish, L. (1969) *The Movies, Mr Griffith and Me*. London: WH Allen.

Marsh, J. and Bearne, E. (2007) *Moving Literacy On*. Leicester: UKLA.

Messaris, P. (1994) *Visual Literacy: Image, Mind, and Reality*. Boulder, CO: Westview Press.

Nowell-Smith, G. and Ricci, S. (eds) (1998) *Hollywood and Europe: Economics, Culture, National Identity 1945–95*. London: British Film Institute.

Ofcom (2008) *Media Literacy Audit: Report on UK Childrens Media Literacy*. Available at www.ofcom.org.uk/advice/media_literacy/medlitpub/medlitpufrss/m/.childrens 08 (retrieved 31 December 2009).

Palmer, S. (2006) *Toxic Childhood: How the Modern World is Damaging our Children and What We Can Do About It*. London: Orion.

Sigman, S. (2005) *Remotely Controlled: How Television is Damaging our Lives*. London: Random House.

UK Film Council (2009) *Statistical Yearbook*. Available at www.ukfilmcouncil.org.uk/yearbook (retrieved 28 December 2009).

Van den. Broek, Paul (2001) 'The Role of Television Viewing in the Development of Reading Comprehension'. Available at www.ciera.org/library/archive/2001-02/04OCT99-58-MSarchive.html (retrieved 28 December 2009).

Resources

Finding Films to Watch

Cary Bazalgette

It is difficult to find really good films that are appropriate for children of primary age and are different from what they are used to. For classroom viewing and discussion, it is more appropriate to use complete short films, rather than clips from feature-length films. There is a much wider range of genres and styles in short films. You will need to have at least some material that you can keep and show repeatedly, rather than just borrowing films on short loan.

The British Film Institute's range of meticulously researched short film anthologies for schools, published between 2001 and 2007, spearheaded the use of high-quality, non-mainstream short films in UK primary schools. *Starting Stories* and *Starting Stories 2* contain films suitable for children of 3+; *Story Shorts* and *Story Shorts 2* are for children of 7+. It should be noted that many of these were not actually made for children, but they are rich enough – as well as short enough – to reward repeated viewing and analysis.

YouTube and other video sharing sites are an obvious place to look for other short films but finding appropriate ones of high quality can be very hard. It is worth looking at websites such as www.vimeo.com: a video-makers' site which prides itself on being 'a respectful community'.

A wealth of feature-length films, as well as shorts, are made for children in Japan, Iran, China, the Nordic countries, Eastern Europe and Latin America. Few are available in the UK, but many are distributed in Europe and the USA. You can buy DVDs with English subtitles from other countries, although if they are Region 1 you will need a DVD player that can show NTSC. When showing films in the UK that do not have a BBFC certificate, you are within your rights legally but it would be sensible to ensure that parents know what you are showing and are happy about it.

Wonderful world cinema titles that you could look out for include the animated Studio Ghibli films from Japan by the director Hayao Miyazaki, such as *Spirited Away, Kiki's Delivery Service* and *My Neighbour Totoro*; Michel Ocelot's animated films *Kirikou et la Sorcière* (set in West Africa) and *Azur et Azmar* (set in North Africa; released in the UK as *The Princes' Quest*); and Iranian live-action films from the 1980s and 1990s such as Abbas Kiarostami's *Where is My Friend's House?* (1987), *Bag of Rice* (Mohammed Ali-Talebi, 1996) and *Children of Heaven* (Majid Majidi, 1997).

(Continued)

(Continued)

For keeping track of what is available, use the European Children's Film Association (ECFA – www.ecfaweb.org) which is the organisation for all who are interested in high-quality films for children and young people. Their journal is free and available online, and is a useful source of information about films that are suitable for children and of high quality.

For a range of older films from the UK and USA as well as world cinema, see the *Watch This!* list of 50 films compiled by the BFI (2008), through a poll of teachers and film education workers around the world, asked to nominate what they thought everyone ought to have seen by the age of 14 – go to www.bfi.org.uk/education/conferences/watchthis/

Part 2
Critical Learning

Children need to gain critical tools with which to analyse the media and to talk and write about them confidently. This kind of learning is important in its own right, but it needs to be embedded in the curriculum, from the first years of schooling.

Rethinking Literacy

Geoff Dean

Chapter objectives

This chapter reviews the history of prejudice that underpins attitudes to non-print media such as pictures and films, and argues for the value of learning about these media in their own right as an integral part of literacy in the 21st century.

This chapter is an argument about literacy, and about attitudes to literacy. At the end of the first decade of the 21st century, increasing amounts of information, stories and ideas are transmitted in non-print forms. A large proportion of that material is carried in moving image texts such as television, film and computer games. Yet anybody searching through the school curriculum currently offered to young learners in school at any phase will discover that there is limited attention given to non-print media except in the specialised 'media studies' context. The most common means by which our population receives the vast majority of its information is almost wholly ignored in the education system.

Of the many anachronisms that still dominate our school systems, one of the biggest is the disproportionate privileging of written word literacy as the centrepiece of educational success and communication. As Pam Czerniewska observes:

> Its privileged status can be recognised in the way that writing is regarded in both teachers' and pupils' minds, as the best way of representing learning. Writing predominates over talk as the proof that learning has taken place and the highest awards go to those who can achieve well on written assignments. Writing and reading are among the major aspects of the child's education that parents are anxious about ... Adults who cannot write are generally considered by themselves and by others as intellectually inferior. (1992: 4)

Of course, it is absolutely essential that all children are taught to read and write in conventional ways: that universal right is not in question. But, just as children are taught to 'make meaning' from the arrangement of sounds, words, sentences and paragraphs in traditional printed texts, so they need to be just as aware of and to understand the arrangement of elements in non-print texts. Being literate today has to include the capacity to notice and understand the composition and framing of shots, the deployment of light, colour and movement, the arrangement of order and duration in aural and visual material; it also needs to include the skills of identifying the sources and reliability of non-print material, and understanding the kinds of truth – and untruth – that can be created through images and sounds.

Much of what currently takes place in schools is based on 19th century principles, through a curriculum model and content that are serviced but not transformed by remarkable technological resources. Yet we need learners who are fully aware of the layers of meaning contained in non-print texts, who quickly and confidently make mature engagements with those texts, and who take from them, to the fullest possible extent, the messages, issues and meanings they convey. In an age when anybody can be a media producer by using a simple facility on their mobile phones, editing easily on laptops and playing the finished product through an MP3 portable player, children need to know the potential of these readily accessible communication tools and the power they contain.

This is recognised by the Cambridge Review of Primary Education in England:

> The more fundamental task [than protection from unsuitable content] is to help children develop the capacity to approach electronic and other non-print media (including television and film as well as the internet) with the degree of discrimination and critical awareness that should attend reading, writing and communicating of any kind. (Alexander, 2009: 270)

By proposing that this capacity should be an essential feature of literacy, the Review presents us with a considerable challenge. What are the barriers that need to be overcome if we are to accept this challenge and rethink literacy for the 21st century? What lies behind the negative attitudes that still prevail towards non-print media in our culture, and what arguments can be mustered to overcome them?

How we have got to where we are

When public schooling became compulsory, as a result of the Forster Education Act of 1870, it was designed (against a background of ruling class disapproval) to service the limited but necessary literacy needs of the industrial revolution. Growing industries required hundreds of thousands of uneducated operatives for menial and boring tasks: to tend the looms, operate the machines, hew at the coal face, and plough the land. The workplace, however, also needed slightly better educated workers to act as clerks, book-keepers and copywriters, administering the orders, adding up the figures, writing the invoices and conducting essential communications between the many industrial enterprises. These requirements led to the devising of a minimalist model of 'literacy' to be delivered through the new school system, designed around rigid criteria, rigorously and systematically monitored by Her Majesty's Inspectorate. Reading and writing were taught in mechanical ways, enabling pupils to make the least possible workable sense of the simplest of texts, and of their Bibles. The written word, once the almost exclusive possession of the rich and powerful, was quickly to become the currency of success in this system. It did not matter that a proportion of the school population would 'fail' in this setting; their future working lives did not depend on literacy skills, and there were plenty of labouring opportunities to occupy them. Pictures and illustrations were playing a bigger part in communicating ideas as popular mass culture blossomed towards the end of the 19th century, but the visual image played a very minor part in the school educational processes of that time.

So the main focus of literacy teaching in primary schools has remained doggedly fixed on the written word ever since. In the years following the First World War, worries began to grow about the new text forms increasingly attracting public interest. Theories about 'dumbing down' have been a concern of the intellectual elite for many decades. As they became more popular, film and advertising, radio and comics, were depicted as enemies of reading, and as appealing only to the lowest possible tastes. Indeed, a few of those issues still preoccupy social commentators and those responsible for educational provision today, the latest scapegoated villain being the computer game and its supposed unregulated intrusion into children's lives. According to its detractors, this activity is bad because it reduces personal reading time, unproblematically regarded as intellectually superior.

A number of regular moral panics about the alleged falling standards of literacy recurred at different periods during the last century. Responsibility for these reductions is often laid directly at the door of new media, all of which are seen as capable of distracting the nation's young from their classroom studies. There is often more than a suggestion that such pastimes are identified as targets for criticism because they have popular appeal in a class-ridden culture. The leisure activities of different social classes have, until modern times, rarely overlapped, as can be quickly shown by some crude stereotypes. In the early years of the 20th century, the middle and upper classes sought their entertainment mostly in the theatre; their working-class counterparts attended music hall shows and the cinema. The middle and upper classes read 'literature'; the working-class reader was more interested in the 'penny dreadful' and illustrated magazines. Not surprisingly, those who could read and write with flourish and acumen thought highly of their advanced abilities, and identified for themselves a jealously guarded sort of 'club'. Literary critics and other taste-formers, particularly academics such as F.R. Leavis (1930) and the Scrutiny group at Cambridge University in the 1930s, argued confidently that certain texts were superior to others, and that there was even a hierarchical scale that could be objectively applied to classical authors. In the early 1930s, Leavis and a colleague, Denys Thompson, were prominent amongst writers responsible for pronouncements about popular culture (1933). Yet, their books and pamphlets were not written to explain new media forms, but to protect the general public from their 'pernicious' influence.

A large part of the population was led to believe, by teachers directly or indirectly influenced by Leavisite thinking, that texts with a high pictorial content were somehow second-rate, less worthy of intellectual attention – and possibly even damaging. So, the reading of comics in school was sneered at, or banned outright. Showing films in the classroom was mostly regarded as a form of babysitting, or sometimes as a 'reward' at the end of a unit of work. Likewise, the watching of television – and more recently, the playing of computer games – have been regularly depicted as a shocking waste of children's valuable time. In modern times, it is not unusual to encounter parents who believe that as soon as their children can decode letters, they should be moved as quickly as possible from picture books to 'chapter' books, in the erroneous belief that the fewer the illustrations, the more challenging the book. Such parents can have no idea how many other layers of meaning are being contributed to those texts through their pictorial content. Pictures and images are often regarded as requiring less mental effort to read effectively, and as likely to stunt the imaginative processes that written text is able to encourage. Pictorial content therefore tends to be regarded as inappropriate and second rate in educational contexts. Primary teachers are usually unaware of the trends in comics being read by their pupils in any generation, and few experienced teachers of English have any sort of contact with or knowledge of the sheer range and scope of graphic novel texts, so popular with many of their male pupils.

Such attitudes doggedly live on. In the summer of 2009, when this chapter was being written, yet another dispute about the study of media texts in schools blew up in the press and broadcast media, fanned by the prejudices and short-sightedness of traditionalist educators. Put simply, their argument is that certain sorts of school subject are more worthwhile and demanding than others (echoing the 1930s' attitudes to 'literature' versus all other published material). Media Studies, or indeed any study of the media, is regarded by those traditionalist individuals as a 'soft' subject, without a significant 'body of knowledge', certainly unworthy to be regarded as a proper test for entrance at the more prestigious universities. This parallels the situation of little more than a hundred years ago, when English was not perceived as a suitable subject for study at Oxford, and had to be made more 'respectable' by the inclusion of a heavy dose of Anglo-Saxon.

Literacy is not just about the written word

In this book, primary teachers are being urged to regard the study of media texts, especially moving image texts, as having the same value and relevance as the study and understanding of word-based texts. Both categories of text are sign and symbol based, and it is necessary in the modern world to be equally fluent in the multiple forms of language through which society communicates with itself.

Before considering the relationship between these different areas of literacy, it is necessary to face and overcome the attitudes outlined above. Teachers have to be offered opportunities to explore and discover for themselves that 'literacy' need not be the increasingly limited notion espoused in the late 1990s by such influential agencies as the National Literacy Strategy, and adopted by most English primary schools. Few schools, despite the wholesale universal adoption of this literacy programme, have ever discussed, analysed or come to any agreements about what they believe actually constitutes 'literacy', or what 'literacy' should mean in their particular circumstances.

A more recent document endorses our proposition that literacy is not just about the written word. Sir Jim Rose, commissioned by the government to review the primary curriculum, noted in his Interim Report (2008):

> The central importance of literacy, generally understood as the ability to read and write, is undeniable. However, the concept of literacy has broadened so that the values, for example, of scientific, technological, mathematical and economic 'literacy' are recognised by society and schools to a far greater extent than ever before. The effects of being 'illiterate' in this broader sense are all too obvious and likely to deepen as the world our children inherit depends increasingly upon understanding in these domains. (para 2.25)

Less than a year later, the term 'media literacy' looked set to acquire a status similar to those 'literacies' listed by Rose, when Secretary of State Ed Balls acknowledged its importance in response to a report on the impact of the commercial world on children's well-being (DCSF, 2009). But, as in Rose's list, the very designation 'media literacy' implies something additional, not integral to literacy itself.

Schools attempting to establish a mature position in regard to the adoption of a definition of literacy could benefit from paraphrasing the Charter for Media Literacy:

> To be media literate means being able to choose and access, understand and analyse, create and express oneself from and in a range of media.

With minimal change, this definition could be helpfully broadened to apply to all texts, and to rethink literacy for our modern age:

> To be literate means being able to choose and access, understand and analyse, create and express oneself from and in a range of texts.

A secure literacy

Virtually every four-year-old child arrives in the classroom with an already well-developed experience of moving images. Nearly all have watched hundreds of hours of moving images in their homes on television or DVD, and possibly at the cinema. Every evening, they will return home to accumulate yet more hours of that experience. Some of the material they encounter will have been produced specifically for their age group, but much will have been originally aimed at adults. Most of those children will own their own collections of favourite texts, including popular animated films such as the *Shrek* or *Toy Story* series, or moving-image products associated with their favourite toys. These DVDs will have been played again and again, and some children will readily quote extracts of the dialogue verbatim, and explain (and quickly locate) their favourite scenes. What most of them will already have begun to understand – as can quickly be established by careful questioning – are aspects of narrative, character, episode and some simple visual conventions. Some will be able to articulate differences between moving-image animated texts and those involving live actors. A few may have begun reflecting on what activities are possible in real life, and what activities are only possible in animated contexts. Shirley Brice Heath reminds us, in her massive social study published in 1983, that 'long before school, their language and culture at home has structured for them the meanings which will give shape to their experiences in classrooms and beyond'. These texts will have been an important funnel for shaping the way that small children encounter and perceive the world, and a school system that respects and caters for the needs of the individual should be capitalising on this knowledge.

Helen Bromley relates an experience that must have been repeated hundreds of thousands of times, in all parts of the country (although DVD has now replaced video for most pre-schoolers):

> The video culture was … much in evidence when I was privileged to make visits to the homes of reception class children. Whatever differences existed between the homes, they all had one thing in common, and that was video ownership. Videos were strewn about the floor, or sat alongside books on shelves or in their own cabinet. In one home Callum was watching *Thomas the Tank Engine* on video, whilst he played the story out in front of the TV with his road mat and toy engines. The story involved a trip to the woods and as Callum played, he related the story of a trip he had made to the woods with his mum, matching the experiences to Thomas's. (1996: 72)

Yet, the majority of teachers fail to take advantage of the invaluable experience children are acquiring at an importantly formative time. Almost immediately on entry, schools prepare pupils for word-based literacy practices, usually ignoring the moving-image based 'literacy' already acquired. But this situation can be changed. Increasing numbers of teachers are gaining confidence in exploring the use of moving-image texts and the equipment that creates them.

A few educationalists have recently made the argument that closer attention to media texts in the early years and primary classrooms is justified, because they know that such study can lead to the enhancement of mainstream word-based literacy. Increasing amounts of research have recently been conducted to explore how the study of pictorial materials can play a positive role. Eve Bearne (Bearne and Wolstencroft, 2007; QCA, 2004, 2005) has conducted a number of studies based on what some educationalists call 'multimodal texts' (posters, non-fiction book illustrations, web pages and graphic stories involving mostly still pictures). With Jackie Marsh, Bearne has also written an important report on the experiences and achievements of primary literacy advisers trained by the British Film Institute to lead on the development of 'moving-image media literacy' in over 60 local authorities. The findings of this research make a strong case for giving greater status to the exploration of moving image as part of the primary curriculum. Positive outcomes from it include:

- Children are usually enthused by watching the text, and concentrate avidly, paying close attention.

- After watching a text, children need little encouragement to begin talking and sharing the experience they have just encountered in extended discourses.

- Whilst watching such texts, children listen very hard and notice much detail about the dialogue, commentary and music, which they remember better from having heard them aloud.

- Watching moving-image texts enables children to think immediately about and notice the ways that settings, characters and plots contribute to meaning – which will all be necessary considerations as the children encounter written narratives.

- Writing linked to moving-image study has shown learners of all ages and abilities to be better motivated, employing a richer use of language and more sophisticated vocabulary, displaying better insight into the motivation and feelings of characters, and prepared to take more risks to bring their writing alive. (Marsh and Bearne, 2008: 22–8).

Conclusion

However, these findings only emphasise the value of learning about non-print media as a support to traditional literacy. The argument needs to be taken further. These media represent key areas of development and understanding in their own right – and are likely to become more essential areas of knowledge as our cultural practices, and the growing ubiquity of technologies, continue to change our relationship with how we employ signs and symbols.

Literacy in this wider sense has a direct relationship with children's lives beyond school. It is only right that they are equipped with the correct tools to make the best sense of the multitude of non-print texts they will continue to encounter. They live in an age in which, as Robert Scholes reminds us:

> ... language and other semiotic systems and their associated media of communication have in the course of history multiplied and penetrated more and more deeply into our daily lives. We are, at present, like it or not, the most mediated human beings ever to exist on this earth ... One needs to be able to read, interpret and criticise texts in a wide range of modes, genres and media. (1998: 84)

This is an enormous challenge to the education system in terms of training and resources, and it is not surprising that policy-makers have resisted its implications. But in the years since Scholes wrote this, we have started to see the development of techniques and approaches that offer teachers simple, practical ways of dealing with non-print texts in the classroom and building them into their literacy teaching. Digital technologies make it increasingly easy to access, study and make non-print texts, both in and out of school. There is a growing body of classroom practice that exemplifies ways of tackling non-print media in the classroom, and increasing numbers of teachers are surprised and delighted by children's responses to a literacy teaching approach that takes their full range of textual experiences into account. The barriers to rethinking literacy, then, are not so much practical and financial as attitudinal. A key element of arguments directed at overcoming these attitudes must therefore be to demonstrate that we have inherited a long tradition of literacy teaching that is grounded in outdated attitudes to class and culture. The first step in rethinking literacy is to give ourselves permission to move on.

References

Alexander, R. (ed.) (2009) *Children, their World, their Education: Final Report and Recommendations of the Cambridge Primary Review*. Abingdon: Routledge.

Bearne, E. and Wolstencroft, H. (2007) *Visual Approaches to Teaching Writing*. London: Paul Chapman Publishing.

Bromley, H. (1996) 'Video narratives in the early years' in Hilton, M. (ed.) *Potent Fictions; Children's Literacy and the Challenge of Popular Culture*. London: Routledge.

Charter for Media Literacy (2004) Available at www.euromedialiteracy.eu (retrieved 30 December 2009).

Czerniewska, P. (1992) *Learning about Writing*. Oxford: Blackwell.

Department for Children, Schools and Families (DCSF) (2009) *Children's Plan Two Years On: Next Steps to Achieve Outstanding Children's Services*. Press release, 14 December 2009, at www.dcsf.gov.uk/pns/DisplayPN.cgi?pn_id=2009_0251 (retrieved 28 December 2009).

Heath, S.B. (1983) *Ways with Words: Language, Life and Work in Communities and Classrooms*. Cambridge: Cambridge University Press.

Leavis, F.R. (1930) *Mass Civilisation and Minority Culture*. Cambridge: The Minority Press.

Leavis, F.R. and Thompson, D. (1933) *Culture and Environment*. London: Chatto and Windus.

Marsh, J. and Bearne, E. (2008) *Moving Literacy On*. Leicester: UKLA.

Qualifications and Curriculum Authority (QCA) (2004) *More than Words: Multimodal Texts in the Classroom*. London: QCA Publications.

Qualifications and Curriculum Authority (QCA) (2005) *More than Words 2*. London: QCA Publications.

Rose, J. (2008) *The Independent Review of the Primary Curriculum: Interim Report*. Teachernet Publications. Available at http://publications.teachernet.gov.uk/eOrdering Download/IPRCReport. pdf (retrieved 10 March 2010).

Scholes, R. (1998) *The Rise and Fall of English*. New Haven, CT: Yale University Press.

Every Picture Tells a Story 2

Geraldine Walker

The aim of this activity is to encourage children to think about how particular elements in any image can be used to help tell a story, and how images in sequence can form the basis of a story. It will also alert children to what needs to be added to images in order to make a satisfactory and believable story.

Download up to 10 images from the web. They could be linked to a specific topic which is being covered in class or they could be totally random.

Photocopy the sheets and give a copy of the images to individuals/pairs/small groups. If the school can afford it, the pictures could be in colour, which is more visually stimulating.

After looking at the images, they need to discuss which pictures they want and then decide which one they will discard in order to make the pictures tell a story.

Glue the remaining images onto paper in order, storyboard style.

When finished, Blu-Tack their storyboards onto the wall.

Each group then takes it in turn to look at the way one or more of the other groups have arranged the images.

Looking at each storyboard, they should note which image has been discarded, which image was used to begin the story with and which was discarded. In each case, they should consider the possible reasons for these choices.

Then – in turn – each group tells their own story to the class. Discuss what needed to be added to the storyboard in words in order to help the story to make sense.

Developments

1. Write the story underneath the images with words or sentences.
2. Repeat the exercise with the same pictures and choose a different image to discard. How does this change the story?
3. Use this as a first draft of a story and begin to expand the work linked to character/description of place/tenses.
4. For children with English as a second language, ask them to tell/write the story in their own language – then write subtitles in English or vice versa.
5. Tell each group which picture they have to start and finish with and see how they arrive at the ending.
6. Turn the story into a short, time-based text. Download the images into software such as Photo Story (available as a free download) or Movie Maker ('bundled' on most PCs).

5

Analysing Advertisements in the Classroom

Shakuntala Banaji

Chapter objectives

This chapter challenges the idea that children are more vulnerable to advertising than adults are, and draws on classroom research to reveal children's awareness of how advertising works and the need for teachers to be clear about the learning outcomes of teaching about advertising.

Assumptions about children and advertising are common: in many academic, school or family settings, it is taken for granted that children are *more vulnerable than adults* to the effects of the media. But, if we view children as being in need of greater protection from advertising than adults, this might mean that we ignore their complex cultural responses to particular advertisements. If we think children are more vulnerable to advertising influences than we are, we might also assume that all children respond in the same ways to advertisements. Unfortunately, and despite the fact that most children live with adults and gain some of their ideas from adults, adults' competence and vulnerability within this same commercial world are less often examined. On the other hand, if we view both children and adults as thoroughly competent consumers, and if advertising is about *nothing but selling products*, then the need to regulate advertisers appears to diminish, and the rationale for teaching about advertisements might be different.

Previous research

Reviewing the research literature on children and advertising, I found very little discussion about precisely how children's thinking in the area of advertising develops. Gunter et al. (2005) argue that the development of children's capacity to think in abstract ways about advertising needs to be factored into discussions of their ability to judge the facts, opinions and persuasive content of advertisements. At the same time, these writers also raise serious concerns about the dangers of drawing general conclusions from studies of children and advertising conducted without careful consideration of the ages and cultural backgrounds of the children interviewed. Sonia Livingstone and Ellen Helsper, however, suggest that 'there is evidence that children of all ages are affected by advertising' (2006: 571). This simple finding should lead those of us who are teachers to further questions of how or even whether children 'of all ages' are more affected by advertising than adults are.

Some researchers suggest that previous studies of children's understanding of advertising messages have relied too heavily on asking children of all ages the same sorts of questions, requiring them to read questionnaires and say or write their answers, in ways that their literacy levels might not support. Owen et al. (2007) argue that younger children may actually be able to think things about advertising that are much more complicated and knowledgeable than the language they are able to use to express their thoughts to others. They also suggest that the way researchers or teachers phrase questions and ideas can be off-putting and confusing for younger children, and can prevent them from expressing the understanding they have.

Teachers therefore need to take care in choosing appropriate methods and materials that will allow children of different ages to express what they think and best show what they understand about advertisements. It is also worth bearing in mind that, as researchers caution, showing an understanding of advertising's intention to persuade does not guarantee that children have an understanding of the complex profit-based factors involved in the relationships between big businesses, consumers or television companies. So, for those of us who believe that teaching about the media has an important contribution to make to children's learning at primary school, how might all these issues be tackled in an age-appropriate manner?

To explore these issues, I undertook a small-scale case study on how two primary schools in vastly differing areas used a pack of advertising-related teaching materials.[1] This was part of a larger evaluation project (Buckingham et al., 2007) in which 'Park Hill Primary' (in an inner-city west London location with a culturally diverse and socially working-class population) was set alongside 'Sea Haven Primary' (in a small town in Kent, with a socially mixed but primarily white English intake). The children were aged nine or ten. The smallness of the sample – a total of 54 children from two classes of 27 – and the short-term nature of the research mean that I can't claim it as representative or draw general conclusions from it. It does, however, provide a snapshot of the many different ways in which culturally varied children *of the same age* engage with similar advertisements. It also reveals the potentials, as well as the pitfalls, of using pre-scripted curriculum materials to approach the topic of advertising.

Teaching advertising: pedagogy, purpose and active learning

I carried out interviews and observations in both schools as a 'participant researcher' over two terms in the spring and summer of 2006. At times, I was a teacher-researcher, facilitating the lessons and questioning children; at others, I was an observer, sitting at the back watching the interactions of children and noting the directions taken by discussion of particular advertisements. I made extensive notes, digital recordings and taped interviews as well as photographs and video data to help me recall and describe the children's perceptions of particular advertisements and their thoughts about advertising in general.

In discussions which took place before the introduction of the teaching pack in both schools, approximately half the children in each class of 27 displayed intermittently what I believe can be regarded as a sophisticated critical understanding of different types of advertising.

They commented on the aim of advertisements and/or their positioning; the selling of ideas; the notion of dissuasion; an awareness of promotional gimmicks; and assessments about how advertisements use visual space in the world at large. Additionally, the possibility of consumer rights, the possibility of advertising hype being misleading, and the issue of redress for such misleading labelling of products were all raised at least once in each group.

Sea Haven Primary: focus-group discussions about the question 'what is advertising?'

Girl 1: I think advertising is where you try to persuade someone to do something, like if you wanted someone to buy an idea or an object, you could use really persuasive words like 'It's the best around', 'you won't find this anywhere else' and –

Girl 2: – yes and then you could also persuade people by asking 'em to try 'em and then if it doesn't work out you get your money back or something ...

Girl 3: And then there's advertising that's trying to persuade someone not to do something.

Girl 1: Yes, like the Road Safety Campaign, *THINK!*

Girl 3: That's trying to persuade you to think and not just run out into the road, so advertising can be about that, like that there are good things, and also to inform you that there are BAD things.

Girl 2: If you don't like something, then it isn't how they say on the ad. Sometimes, things aren't how they say they are, they are bad.

Girl 1: And sometimes advertising can be trying to persuade you to do something or not to do something, not just to *buy* some product.

Arising from the class discussion, the teacher noted the following points mentioned by the children:

- advertising is everywhere

- it is often eye-catching and sometimes shocking or scary

- it persuades you to do something or to buy something

- it tries to sell a product

- it can try to 'sell' an idea not a product

- it can try to dissuade as well as persuade

- it can inform or sell, it does not have to sell

- it can be written or spoken or visual or all three

- it may be found in a whole range of places, from newspapers, bus hoardings, product packets and television to supermarkets, the radio and the internet

- it can use writing or music or visuals or spoken words.

During several initial discussions, I observed confusion about liking an advertisement as against liking a product. This distinction is one that is often ignored in studies of advertising and young children. Indeed, the multimodal pleasures of advertising are frequently ignored in favour of a content-focused approach, which seeks to prove or dis-prove negative effects. During this study, most children were open about having their thoughts on specific subjects altered in specific, usually time-limited ways by particular advertisements; however, fur-ther extensive discussions revealed that this 'effect' was also usually related to an existing partiality for the product (not the brand) arising from experience or from discussions with friends and parents. All of this is not that dissimilar to the way in which most adults relate to advertisements and products. We should remember, additionally, that many children also report finding advertisements irritating when they interrupt programmes they are enjoying. Several reported that younger siblings would start to cry or misbehave during advertising breaks in programmes, and there was little evidence of any inability to judge the difference between entertainment and advertising content.

When the teaching materials were introduced, the children were soon highly engaged in discussions about *competition* between differ-ent products. However, in Park Hill particularly, this was understood (or misconstrued) as being based on actual product features, rather than as an aspect of advertising rhetoric. Another issue was highlighted by children's sharply different reactions to the OXO soup cube ad campaign. At least 15 claimed that they did not like it. This was mainly because it was seen as depicting a white middle-class family, and as making people from 'other cultures' seem strange or exotic. This resistance came as a surprise to the teacher, who in response attempted to emphasise the 'healthy eating' and 'multicultural food' aspects of the campaign, thus showing that teaching about advertising can involve a complex balance for adults too, between displaying cultural competence and undertaking textual critique.

Comments by a range of children showed a multiplicity of perspectives, ranging from 'What's the joke?' when watching the OXO family tease a father for keeping a picture of a female pop icon in his wallet, through 'How is it healthy to boil all the vegetables so much? Doesn't it kill all the vitamins? That's what our teacher told us' to 'That's not *real* Chinese/curry/Italian' or 'I wouldn't be able to digest my food if my parents were touching each other like that' or 'I'd never speak to my parents like that; I'd get beats'. Many researchers might have ignored or passed over these responses as aberrant readings, or missed them altogether because of the seeming naturalisation of whiteness both for advertisers and for researchers in this area (Burton, 2009). That several of the children viewed the OXO advertisements as part of an alien narrative, to be critiqued and distrusted, was clearly the opposite of the advertisers' intentions. Had the advertisements not been explored within the educational space of the classroom and time for such discussion provided, such critiques would not have been articulated; nor would the teacher have known that a critical stance to advertising existed alongside what he decried as the children's 'brand-obsessed' culture.

In terms of the design and content of advertising-related teaching materials for primary-age children, the reaction sparked by the OXO ads had several implicit pedagogic repercussions. Many of the children in the ethnically diverse school did not relate to the advertisements depicting monolithic cultural spaces, and were disengaged during their viewing, while in Sea Haven, the preponderance of white children made the scenarios portrayed more familiar. Some children's dismissive reception of certain advertisements, and their jokey recasting of the supposed 'messages', almost pitched the teacher into the role of justifying these advertisements that were failing to captivate them. In line with this finding about openness of interpretation within the child audience when faced with advertisements without adult framing, teaching materials using closed approaches such as the sentences: 'the most important shot in the ad is' … and 'the message of the ad is …' are dangerous in their tendency to accept the advertisement's message on its own terms, thereby inhibiting children's own interpretations.

Concomitantly, it can be seen to be crucial to children's understanding if teachers are willing to experiment and allow open-ended activities that do not simply rely on a skills-based notion of acquiring proficiency in the language of advertising as it already exists. During the production of storyboards for an imaginary Fish OXO cube in Park

Hill, instead of using the teaching materials' designated cut-and-paste activity that would leave the white middle-class OXO family intact, children who were dissatisfied with the original campaign were encouraged to design alternatives. Some of the ideas that came out clearly showed differences in culture and values at work in the reception of advertisements, while also demonstrating serious technical learning taking place in relation to the use of different shot types, humour, lighting, camera angles and edits. For example, a storyboard for Fish OXO presented to the class by two Moroccan boys was based on a situation in one of their households. All the other storyboards were interesting but the class voted this one the best, based on a combination of humour and the success of its persuasive message:

Shot 1: medium long shot, a room, with dim light, father and son sitting at opposite ends of a bed watching television.

Shot 2: son is cooking, father watching TV.

Shot 3: close up: father looking sad.

Shot 4: close up: son looking sad.

Shot 5: close up: son crumbles Fish OXO cube into the pot.

Shot 6: father and son sitting facing each other smiling, eating Fish OXO meal.

Shot 7: big close up: Fish OXO cube – SLOGAN: *Little Cube: Big Smile.*

In another much-liked ad, two toddler twins were shown going missing. Their parents searched for them frantically. At the end of the storyboard, the toddlers had laid the table themselves and called their parents for dinner. The slogan read 'Fish OXO – so simple even your baby can use it'.

Again, teachers need to be aware that by sticking mechanically to curriculum materials, they may close down on imaginative reinterpretation if they simply use the one-size-fits-all tasks provided. The use of cut-and-paste stills from an original advertisement actually discourages such innovative and alternative perspectives as the ones described here.

A comment by one of the teachers in Park Hill shows that teacher expectations of quiet or low-achieving children are challenged by their creative production work:

The few children that I thought wouldn't be engaged at all, were actually the ones that were the most eager. I was so surprised. Even though a few had to be moved, after that they were really interested and took a really active role. So clearly this type of media work appeals to them and plays to their strengths. (Teacher)

In this regard, a simulation activity, the making of an advertising campaign for the school using digital cameras, drew in the children for whom speaking English proved challenging. The planning and framing of shots or sequences, the attendant praise when a shot came out well, and the contribution their efforts made to a group result were crucial in raising confidence. These are features of media production work that are transferable across genres and could be linked to the teaching of film or television. Some teachers prefer to avoid advertising in the classroom on the grounds that, as one told me, 'they get enough of that rubbish at home'. However, consciously teaching about advertising with primary school children can stimulate discussions that would not otherwise have taken place. Particularly in relation to non-commercial advertising – perceived as being more about *ideas* than *products* – the children in this study revealed a sophisticated grasp of intention and emotional content:

Boy 1:   I started watching advertisements quite young, I think maybe three years old with my parents.

Boy 2:   Me too.

Interviewer: Any particular ones you want to talk about?

Boy 3:   I remember these ones about a kid getting kicked by his dad. You might've started to watch it, yeah, and not known what it was about and kept watching.

Boy 2:   Yeah, right, it was scary, I mean, for little children; they might've not known it was an advertise. Child abuse [very soft].

Boy 4:   That's what the advertise company wants! To make it seem real. In that the kid is in the corner, and his dad is just coming towards him, to hit him, and … it's about child violence, and it's telling us that this happens, this is real so give money to help these children … It's no use if none of us gives money. It's about making us aware.

Boy 1:   But they shouldn't've gone so far, I don't think. With the kid, and in this with the axe and the legs and all. It could give small kids nightmares …

Interviewer: Small kids? I noticed that a lot of you flinched. Does that make it a less or more effective ad would you say?

Boy 4:   But sometimes it has to be like that, to have an impact. Otherwise no one would do anything.

Interviewer: But do you think that some advertisements do go too far and show things that they should not, given that they are going to be watched by children?

Boy 2: Yes.

Boy 1: Yes, but like he says, it's like that to make us think. Make us do something, or not do something. Like I really like the Nicorette ones, with the cigarettes lying everywhere it's *so disgusting* but when I watch that I never want to smoke. And I want everyone to stop.

This extended discussion with its references to 'impact'– both positive and negative – to shock tactics, to motivation and action as well as the protective stance towards younger children, suggests that discussions of *effects* also need to focus more on non-commercial advertising, which is often simply ignored in the rush to relate all advertising effects to the commercial world.

What is learnt is not always what is taught

The teachers involved reported 'success' in teaching about advertising in terms of children becoming more aware of the persuasive appeals of advertising, their use of 'media language' (such as camera work and music), and awareness of how consumers are targeted in both commercial and non-commercial advertising. Furthermore, teachers viewed advertising literacy as important due to their perceptions of advertisements as a powerful influence not only on children but also on their parents. The children, on the other hand, were attracted by the idea of knowing technical details about camera techniques, and by the opportunities for discussion and practical work. The participant observations showed that these 10-year-olds already possessed considerable general knowledge about advertising, and were positive and enthusiastic about discussing particular advertisements. A number of children certainly were confused about the association between a product and the endorser, or between one product and another when one was being used to enhance the appeal of the other. Perhaps most important was the observation that some children were culturally and/or socially alienated by the authentic advertisements in the teaching materials, drawn from the UK media. Where the pedagogy allowed for open-ended discussions, the children began to develop critiques of the ads' representations of race, childhood and class. However, there were occasions when the materials used did not aid such discussion, but rather lent themselves to didactic and text-centred teaching, thus silencing some children's experiences and knowledge, and holding back the learning of others.

Conclusion

There is still little agreement amongst policy-makers, academics and researchers about the complicated ways in which children from different cultural contexts relate to and interact with the ideas and representations in advertisements. This lack of understanding is not good, either for children or for adults. I have attempted to shed light on a number of questions: What kind of cultural learning takes place when children from different backgrounds interact with advertisements? Do children see advertisements merely as vehicles for products or do they serve other functions in children's cultural lives? And what kind of media literacy work, if any, might enable children to (a) challenge social and cultural representations within the advertisements they watch on a daily basis and (b) feel comfortable about the pleasures (e.g. humour and music) on offer in some advertisements?

In the time-constrained context of real classrooms, we often choose to ignore what we all know: that children learn a lot more when they are actively engaged in doing or making something rather than simply in discussing or answering questions. Sadly, production work, with all the mess and noise it brings during the planning, negotiation and execution stages, appears in most cases to be somewhat stifled by more controlled primary school environments. But where it *is* carried out, it is one of the most successful aspects of teaching and learning about advertising, and facilitates different kinds of learning and success for children sidelined by those who place their emphasis mainly on talk or writing that displays 'media' or 'consumer' literacy.

Children's increasing sophistication in their thinking about advertising and advertisements needs to be explored at different ages, and through methods that do not confuse or exclude certain children, particularly in the younger age groups. We also need to be clear about the reasons for teaching about advertising. Do we want to train children to be discerning consumers, or do we want to rescue them from consumerism, to inoculate them, by exposing the worthlessness of particular products or the duplicitous motives of advertisers? To answer the question in the title of this chapter, it is important for us as teachers not to detach advertisements from the contexts in which they are made and interpreted. Helping children to be 'Adwise' involves approaching advertisements as complicated social and media texts, unpicking their narratives in the way we might unpick written fiction. It can also involve inviting children to consider related questions about other forms of persuasion (for instance, within families or by politicians), about justice and inequality.

Note

1. See Buckingham et al. (2007). Note that a new approach to teaching about advertisements underpins Media Smart's latest set of free resources, *Digital Adwise*, at http://digitaladwise.mediasmart.org.uk (retrieved 9 January 2010).

References

Buckingham, D., Willett, R., Banaji, S. and Cranmer, S. (2007) *Media Smart Be Adwise 2: An Evaluation*. Available at www.mediasmart.org.uk/teachers-research.php (retrieved 9 January 2010).

Burton, D. (2009) '"Reading" whiteness in consumer research', *Consumption Markets and Culture*, 12 (2): 171–201.

Gunter, B., Oates, C. and Blades, M. (2005) *Advertising to Children on TV: Content, Impact and Regulation*. Mahwah, NJ: Lawrence Erlbaum.

Livingstone, S. and Helsper, E. (2006) 'Does advertising literacy mediate the effects of advertising on children? A critical examination of two linked research literatures in relation to obesity and food choice', *Journal of Communication*, 56 (3): 560–84.

Owen, L., Auty, S., Lewis, C., and Berridge, D. (2007) 'Children's understanding of advertising: an investigation using verbal and pictorially cued methods', *Infant and Child Development*, 16 (6): 617–28.

Points for Practice

Reading Images 2

Cary Bazalgette

1. **Complete the image**
   Select an interesting image and show just half of it on the interactive whiteboard (IWB), or give each child half of a photo from a newspaper or magazine, stuck to a larger sheet of plain paper. Their job is to draw in what they think is in the other half – either as a collective exercise on the IWB, taking it in turns to draw in one feature or item, or to do it as individuals or in pairs, working on paper. The exercise requires the children to think carefully about what they can see in the half they do have, and to speculate imaginatively about what might be in the other half. Poor drawing skills do not matter: it's observation and imagination that count.

2. **Uncover the image (IWB only)**
   Instead of projecting the whole image right away, use the IWB tools to expose just a small area. First, ask the children to say what they can see (you may need to push them for detail), then to guess what might be in the rest of the picture. Then expose a little more (or ask a child to decide which bit to expose) and go through the same process. Try not to make this into a guessing game with the aim of getting it 'right', but keep focused on the children's imaginative and observational skills. Use prompt questions such as 'why did you want to open up that part next?' It is fun when the whole image is finally exposed if you have chosen images that include surprising but telling details.

3. **Captions**
   The caption to a photograph 'anchors' the meaning of an image and encourages you to 'read' it in a particular way. So start by going through the kind of analysis suggested in 'Reading Images 1' (page 25) without any captions; then, as a final task, ask children to devise their own captions for the image. This could be done individually or in pairs or groups. Each caption can then be shown next to the image and its effects discussed. The aim is to get children to see that each caption can change the way they interpret an image, by drawing attention to some features and away from others.

4. **Music**
   This has a similar aim to the caption exercise but enables children to see how a choice of music can change the way an image is interpreted. If you

(Continued)

(Continued)

use Photostory 3 or similar software, you can also use the 'pan' or 'zoom' options to move across the image while the music plays, providing a sense of narrative. Children's choices about which tool to use and how to move it, would be important. With access to a number of computers, they could also work on this individually or in small groups.

5. **What happens next?**
   Having studied a still image, ask children to discuss or think about what might happen next, and to describe or draw the 'next image'. This is different from writing a whole story: you are simply asking them to use what they have observed in the first image, as a basis for devising the second.

6

A Learning Journey

Christine Whitney

Chapter objectives

This chapter describes how learning about moving-image media has become established in Lincolnshire schools, and how teachers can move on from seeing film as a stimulus to 'traditional' literacy, to recognising the continuities between all forms of expression.

As a classroom practitioner, I had for many years planned for and embraced the engagement of learners that came with working on moving-image media. What I had not explored fully at that time were the possibilities, way beyond film as stimulus, which this medium could provide. This chapter traces that learning journey for me as I began to explore the role of moving-image texts in relation to print-based texts, and to what were then the prevailing approaches to reading and writing in schools.

My early work with film sprang from the belief that in order to connect with not only the children I taught but also the parents, I needed to link into the texts that children were 'actively reading' at home (Browne, 1999; Meek, 1991) and bring these into the classroom. If our youngest children have, by the age of three, 'learned the codes and conventions through which moving images tell stories' (BFI Education/ DfES, 2003), then this must be capitalised upon and developed in our primary schools.

The Lincolnshire project

Belief in this principle lent strong persuasiveness to my pitch, and led to a small-scale project with 15 schools in Lincolnshire in 2006. The initial aim was to raise standards in reading and writing by working with film as text and by making connections between directorial and authorial intent, examining the symbiotic communicative processes of both print-based and audio-visual text. The following year, the project widened to reach 20 schools, and later, as a result of promising data from the primary years, expanded to cover some 26 Lincoln city primary and nursery schools. In its fourth year, the project was extended to the south of this large rural county. The aim remained to engage practitioners in developing the use of the moving image and the language of film, in order to motivate children, maximise their potential and assist them in their learning journeys as both viewers and authors.

Participating teachers remarked on how working with film can engage and motivate all learners:

> This work (with film) has opened a door for him to achieve. (Teacher of six-year-old child)

> Children are more enthusiastic to write – with more detail and improved structure – and there is an increased enthusiasm among boys. (Teacher working with the 7–11 age group in one of our project schools)

Yet to use film only as stimulus would be to deny the potential of the moving image for developing skills, such as textual exegesis and narrative composition, that are relevant to any medium. Conveying this message to teachers who felt constrained by the National Curriculum and by the demands of tests linked to school 'league tables' posed a challenge.

In order for Heads to accept the programme of continuing professional development (CPD) offered in our project, it had to be initially rooted in raising standards; and it had to be possible to provide it within the confines of the National Curriculum and the objectives of the Primary Framework (a national policy with detailed guidelines and objectives for literacy in primary schools) (DCSF, 2008). This however was never seen as a constraint in our project; rather, it was an opportunity to show that film text had a rightful place alongside print-based text, and that film-making, however time-consuming initially, would illuminate process and structure in written composition as well. This led to specific objectives, relating to text on screen, being incorporated into the national Primary Framework; and many of the objectives relating to creating and shaping text, and reading for meaning, can now be taught in any school through the medium of film.

This now means that whatever CPD we deliver in our schools within the field of the moving image, sits comfortably also within the National Curriculum and the Primary Framework's objectives and units of work. Moving image education is thus integrated into the Primary Framework in our project schools.

Critical analysis of film

If we are to build upon the knowledge, garnered by pre-school children, of the codes and conventions through which moving images tell stories, then CPD for teachers and practitioners needs to start here – with CPD for teachers on critical analysis of film. This means looking behind the surface of the screen to understand a film's intentions, techniques and qualities. Discussing the ways that films are put together, examining decisions made by the director about camera angles or to what effect a close-up has been used, are all useful methods through which to evaluate the effect of a text on the viewer. This critical understanding can be transferred across different modes and media and so impacts on a child's understanding of print-based text.

The British Film Institute (BFI) has produced a model for critical analysis of moving-image texts (BFI Education, 2004), which we use in our CPD along with their short film compilations. This model includes taking a range of narrative features and production devices used in moving-image texts, as starting points for analysis and discussion. They can be grouped into two categories: Cultural Codes which are common to both filmed and written texts, and Technical Codes, which are used only in moving-image media:

For example, in a session with a class of six-year-olds, focusing on the ways sound was used in a particular film, one responded to questions

Cultural codes	Technical codes
Character	Cutting (Editing)
Setting	Camera shot and angle
Story	Colour
Sequence	Sound
Symbol	Composition
Category (Genre)	

Figure 6.1   A range of narrative features and production devices

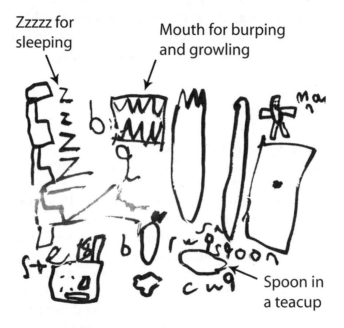

Figure 6.2   A child's response to a soundtrack

about what he imagined was happening in the film as he listened to the opening minute of the soundtrack. At this stage in his development, the most appropriate way for him to respond was by drawing on his individual whiteboard, as reproduced in Figure 6.2.

His teacher later commented that listening to the soundtrack had helped him to make predictions in Guided Reading (an approach to teaching reading where children's learning is scaffolded in a small group situation and they are supported to reach the next steps on their journey to become independent readers).

What is it about listening to a soundtrack that stimulates such a powerful response in young children? It may be the multi-sensory composition that enables children to make inferences beyond what they are able to do with print-based texts. Teachers tell us that children seize opportunities for talk and discussion to a greater extent after viewing films. After working with film, young children offer responses that include a rich use of adjectival language: such responses are not elicited to the same extent after reading print-based text. The audio-visual element is all important in carrying meaning to the child.

In the same class, a teacher spent some time examining and discussing framing and composition in the film *Baboon on the Moon* (Duriez 2002, in *Starting Stories*, BFI Education, 2004). In response to a question about why the Earth was out of focus in one particular shot, the child replied:

> Baboon is sad because he misses his mummy and daddy. He wants to go home but the Earth is too far away to get there. He plays a sad song to let mum and dad know that he is sad and on the moon.

For this child, learning was not a matter of naming the type of shot or camera angle; rather, it was about decoding the language of film and applying it to his knowledge of the title character in order to make meaning. It is paramount in our work with film that we teach not only the inherent codes and conventions but also how these relate to an overall understanding of text, whether print or film based.

For 7- to 11-year-olds, this decoding of film texts goes beyond 'spot the shot' analysis to developing critical understanding through a teacher's skilful questioning. For example, teachers are beginning to use film texts in their Guided Reading, relating directorial intent and purpose to authorial intent and purpose. Stills are taken from the film and used as a basis for discussion and for developing critical response. There may be an initial question relating to camera angle but that line of questioning is taken further as children relate the specific shot or angle to meaning, and to directorial intent. Once children begin to create film themselves, they see and feel the need to make decisions about framing and composition. Here again we see that the decon-struction of text is inextricably linked to creative production.

Deepening understanding through creative work

It remains necessary to make clear the symbiotic communicative processes of both print-based text and moving-image text. Much of a film's story is told through types of shot, and their juxtaposition. In making links between critical analysis and writing, the project asks the question 'how can we achieve the same effect in writing as the film produces in the viewer when all we have are words?' Practitioners are trained through the project's extensive CPD package in how to make the links between the two modes of communication. Details may be picked out from a close-up in a film and translated into writing, into adjectival or adverbial phrases or precise nouns.

It is not particularly the writing for or within the film that works to improve children's writing, nor simply the film as stimulus; rather, it is the deeper understanding of the needs of the viewer and therefore the intent of the film-maker, which has had an impact, as teachers have seen the benefit of children making a short film as a learning outcome within a Primary Framework unit or in other National Curriculum programmes of study.

A class of six-year-olds was working on a non-fiction unit, which required from them a non-chronological report on rattlesnakes. The children researched their topic, through paper- and screen-based texts, formulating questions as they investigated: where do rattlesnakes live? What do rattlesnakes eat? They then decided to use their knowledge to make a three-minute film as their way of answering these and other questions. Using stop frame animation, video and home-made sound effects, they did precisely that, producing a short film in which the textual organisation and linguistic features of a non-chronological report were fully reflected.

Alongside the growing use of small, handheld video cameras to create short film narratives or non-fiction sequences, there comes a related impact on understanding about content and structure. The addition of sound aids an understanding of how to create atmosphere and mood, or how to use dialogue to move a story forward. In the same way, film-editing software supports the structuring of text. In supporting teachers with their creative practice in the making of film as outcome or as process, we offer a means of scaffolding learning, especially in relation to writing skills. For example, a class of seven-year-olds may begin a film narrative about St George and The Dragon using flashback at the moment the sword pierces the dragon's skin. As a print-based literacy objective, something like this would not be taught until much later. In relation to film, it is possible to teach and model learning objectives far beyond those deemed appropriate to the same age in relation to print.

> Children are achieving aspects of sub-levels several jumps ahead. (Teacher remarking on the effect of working with film in her class)

Embedding film in the curriculum

As schools become more knowledgeable about moving-image education, we have witnessed the progression from film being used to support reading and writing in Literacy, to working with film across the whole primary curriculum. For example, film was initially used solely within Literacy as an alternative to print-based text, as an 'on-screen' text. We now see teachers throughout the school working with the moving image: children in Science use simple animation to explain their understanding of how a circuit works; in Primary Languages, they offer a simple narrative in French; in History, they seek to explain how the Fire of London began. In all these cases, children's understanding of the language features of specific text types and genres is deepened and transferred as the film is composed and reviewed. Recently, the making of a short film about how to attract wild birds into the garden through making a bird-seed feeder required, as a corollary, proficiency in instructional writing. This led to children, at the editing stage, listening to their soundtrack and realising that their instructions would not be clearly understood. So they reworked the audio element, looking again at their written text until they were satisfied that the viewer would know exactly what to do.

The CPD offered for the overall project was received with enthusiasm by most teachers as this 'new way of looking at film' (as opposed to the old approach of comparing a book with the-film-of-the-book) lent a new excitement to what for many had become a 'safe', monochrome approach to teaching. One commented: 'I'm looking at film in a different way now.'

Film in the nursery class

For a minority of teachers, however, the thought of changing the way they had been teaching, or learning how to use a camera, or learning how to 'read' film all seemed too daunting. In an interview, one class teacher spoke frankly about her initial feelings as her school began the project:

> When I was told that we were going to have to introduce visual literacy and do filming with nursery children, my heart sank and I thought, 'oh no, another initiative'. I was dreading it. I thought I really have got to the end of my career and I can't do this any more. But when I tried the Baboon film with my children for the first time and used the method of play, pause, talk to the children, get them to predict, play all the way through I couldn't believe how enthralled the children were and how interested. There was no dialogue but they were glued … and it just took off from there.

After several weeks, she was asked once more about her opinions on working with the moving image, and responded, 'I think it's wonderful! It didn't just inspire the children, it inspired me'.

The teacher in question was supported in the project by a local authority Literacy consultant. Although the teacher had initially been adamant that this approach would not work with pre-school children, the consultant set up an initial viewing of *Baboon on the Moon,* inviting parents, carers and siblings. After repeated viewings with the teacher, the children decided to invite Baboon (the main character) to live with them in the nursery. They felt that in this way they could become Baboon's friends and solve the problem of his perceived loneliness, which they inferred from the film's emotionally powerful though unresolved ending – a narrative type not often experienced by children of this age. Their affective response, shown through their concern for his welfare, led them to construct a rocket for him so that he could travel back to Earth and see his family once more. The children talked about what they would need to provide for Baboon and looked closely at what was in each frame in order to build him a home in their role-play area. They looked carefully at the events in Baboon's day, sequencing them still by still, and made a decision that they wanted to recreate not only his home but also his work place. With their teacher, they created a list of items needed, then worked together to paint an outer space background and a moonscape for Baboon to walk on. This provided opportunities for teamwork, creativity and the development of fine motor skills.

Similarly, role play, arising out of the film, had a positive effect on the children's willingness to collaborate. The class teacher said:

> Working with the film helped with their co-operative play because it gave them a theme they could follow; there was a story line they all knew. It meant

they were able to think of new things to say to each other to follow or to extend the story. Previously if they were playing in the role-play area we'd have had a lot of parallel play and only occasionally would they join in with each other. But because they know it is Baboon's house it has united them all and has really developed their co-operative play.

Following this, one father in discussion with his child about how sad Baboon was, created a 'Baboon computer game', the aim being to find a friend for Baboon so that he would not be sad. Another parent offered to make a fabric book with the children about Baboon, using different methods of fastening. Yet another parent sent in photographs of the moon, after spending time looking out at space, through his telescope, with his daughter, 'to see if they could find Baboon'. A noticeboard was placed outside the nursery door, where specific news about what was happening in Baboon's world was posted daily.

Role-play areas stimulated by books are a normal part of pre-school and infant classrooms. So how did the role play differ here when the stimulus was a moving-image text rather than a written text? I believe, firstly, that connections were made with the world of the children through a medium with which they were familiar and whose codes they had already begun to interpret. No decoding of words acted as a barrier – the children read the visuals, saw the main character, saw where he lived and his daily routine. They were instantly transported to his world, and once his world came to them in the shape of the role-play area, he could come to live among them and they too could inhabit his world. They had an affective response to the film – they became concerned for Baboon's welfare and built a rocket for him to travel back to Earth. Everything they saw and heard within the frame, coupled with the open-ended narrative, worked to make the role play an integral part of the study of this film at pre-school level.

The children continued to 'play' with Baboon and accept him into their world. He became the focus for a themed unit of work the next term on 'The Jungle' as the children decided it was time to take him home and see where he originally lived. My lasting memory of this class and their response to the film came on a final visit to the school two terms later. This time the role-play area had become a doctor's clinic and, behind a desk, complete with white coat and stethoscope, sat Dr Baboon – a large four-foot-high, stuffed model made by a parent for the children of the class. Not only were the teacher's attitude and practice transformed but so also were her ICT knowledge and skills, when for the first time she gave a presentation to other nursery teachers, telling them about her journey with film.

Conclusion

My own journey of exploration continues as I seek to see moving-image education embedded in the primary curriculum as an entitlement for all children and as a teaching and learning tool for all teachers. Film undoubtedly does provide stimulus, engagement and motivation, but it is the opportunity to develop an understanding of the grammar of film and its relationship to print-based texts that I am exploring now.

References

BFI Education/DfES (2003) *Look Again! A Teaching Guide to Using Film and Television With Three- to Eleven-year-olds*. London: British Film Institute.

BFI Education (2004) *Starting Stories*. London: British Film Institute.

Browne, N. (1999) *Young Children's Literacy Development and the Role of Televisual Texts*. London: Falmer Press.

Chambers, A. (1996) *Tell Me: Children Reading and Talk*. Oxford: Oxford University Press.

Department for Children, Schools and Families (DCSF) (2008) *Primary Frameworks*. Available at www.standards.dfes.gov.uk/primaryframework/literacy (retrieved 3 January 2010).

Meek, M. (1991) *On Being Literate*. London: Bodley Head.

Points for Practice

Talking about a Film

Cary Bazalgette

Film viewings should be set up so that every child can see the screen well, and you can see them. It may be better to group children on chairs or on the floor, rather than sitting at desks or tables around the room. It is important to have good external speakers and to make sure that the sound can be heard properly. You should always preview whatever you are going to show. Establish a standard of behaviour for film viewing: full attention and no chattering.

Films that are different from what children are used to may need some preparatory work or discussion.

Drawing out existing, unarticulated knowledge in discussion after a film viewing requires a different pedagogic approach from what some teachers are used to.

It's essential to ask open questions, not anticipating children's responses with loaded questions like 'what did you like best?' and not asking children to guess what's in your mind. Examples of open questions are:

1. Was there anything you enjoyed in this film?
2. Was there anything you didn't like?
3. Was there anything that puzzled you?
4. Was there anything that was different from other films you have seen?
   (Questions taken from a BFI/CLPE adaptation of Aidan Chambers' (1996) 'tell me' questions)

It's important to listen properly to what children say, and to use follow-up questions that challenge them to refine and extend their responses, such as 'how could you tell?' or 'what made you think that?' It is unhelpful to give the impression that there is a 'right answer' by responding with comments like 'good!' and 'that's right!' There may be different interpretations and preferences: this should be explored as an interesting phenomenon, rather than seeking consensus. Different interpretations can motivate a re-viewing of the film – another reason for selecting complete short films rather than clips for classroom study.

For more extended work on a film, children's powers of inference can be stimulated by playing a short sequence of soundtrack only, or just the opening minute of a film, and then inviting comment, before watching the rest (see also 'Film Adaptations', page 100).

(Continued)

(Continued)

The introduction of specialist language such as 'close-up' or 'tracking shot' can support children's interpretations and encourage their further exploration, but the mastery of technical terms should not be a teaching objective in itself. Identifying filmic devices should follow from children's interpretations and your own follow-up questions ('what made you think that?'), which should then lead you back to the film – if necessary using the pause button at key moments – to identify exactly what they saw. *Making Movies Make Sense* from Media Education Wales is an excellent resource to help children aged 9 and older understand these terms (see www.mediaedwales.org.uk/pagesEnglish/ resources/MakingMMS.htm).

Part 3

Creative Learning

Learning about the media needs to include opportunities for creative activities. These do not always have to be ambitious projects, but can be a normal part of everyday learning.

7

Helping Children Tell the Stories in their Heads

Becky Parry

Chapter objectives

Focusing on a 10-year-old boy with poor writing skills but extensive knowledge and understanding of comics, films and computer games, this chapter explores the differences between filmic and written texts and how these can create barriers to learning if they are not understood by both teachers and learners.

> I can think of a story in my head. But I'm not that good at writing. (Connor, aged 10)

What constitutes a good story? What is considered good story writing in school? And what happens when children encounter a literacy curriculum which seems to be at odds with their own experiences of narrative from films, games and cartoons? In this chapter, I will offer some answers to these questions, based on observations of one child, Connor, who I encountered during my research on the role of film and media in developing children's understandings of narrative.

Connor's knowledge of film

Within minutes of starting my first session with the class from which I was going to select a focus group, I had learnt Connor's name and realised that he had already been contemplating some of my research questions:

> I think all children's films have a message, Miss, a moral at the end. Do you?

Later, he responded to a clip from the opening scene of the film *Mirrormask* (dir. McKean, UK/USA, 2005), by saying:

> Well I think that girl is going to be the main character, the one we see in the first shot and the rest of the film will be about her problem and how she solves that problem.

Connor was clearly able to apply his knowledge of children's films to an unfamiliar text, i.e. that often the main character is shown in close-up in the earliest moments of the film, that she has a problem and that the film will conclude by solving the problem. Most children instinctively infer this as they watch and develop an understanding of films, but Connor was spontaneously able to make this understanding explicit.

Discussing with the class teacher which children I might select for the focus group, she surprised me by saying that Connor, although a popular member of the class, often became detached from classroom activity and had never responded like that to a group discussion activity before. He was under-achieving in literacy, something she attributed to his home circumstances.

In discussions with Connor, it became clear that film, for him, was not background wallpaper, something to pass the time. It was an important part of the structure of his life. He described it as part of a routine: taking part in sport after school, watching television, having his tea and then, before bedtime, watching films. He named two he had recently watched: *Wedding Crashers* (dir. Dobkin, USA 2005) and *Cool Runnings* (dir. Turteltaub, USA 1993), both of which were screened on television in the week prior to the first interview. Neither is specifically a children's film and neither is a popular, contemporary film targeted at 10-year-old boys. Connor regularly made his own decisions about what he watched. He commented on a number of occasions that he didn't just watch something because it was on.

He didn't flick channels; he noticed if there was a film on he wanted to watch and then set aside time to watch it. Similar behaviour with books would be perceived by many as highly desirable literacy-related activity.

One of Connor's favourite films was *Toy Story* (dir. Lasseter, USA 1995), which had become an aspect of his 'ongoing' identity (Giddens, 1991: 54): 'I'll always like *Toy Story*. I know that, because it's a good film.' He used the word 'always' here in a nostalgic manner, acknowledging that he had moved on but that the film had a status as the source of a story his mum told about him as a child. At the time of the first interview, his taste had changed and to illustrate this he used *High School Musical* (dir. Ortega, USA 2006) which he said had real people in and was about dancing. Connor's love of film was matched with his love of street dance, and school was an outlet for this interest. By the second phase in the project, when the group were devising ideas for their own film, he had rejected *High School Musical* for films such as *Save the Last Dance* (dir. Carter, USA 2001) and *Step Up* (dir. Fletcher, USA 2006), which he perceived as more mature, while still about real people, difficult situations and dance. Like a reader of books, he sought out new film experiences because he had outgrown the ones he'd already 'read'.

Connor and narrative

Connor regularly talked about being able to see stories in his head:

C: It was about these two boys, brothers, and they had a real dad who was a yoga master. Anyway it was one of the boys' birthdays. They were twins. A big storm blew up and the two boys were separated. The father died. Then it was about seven years later and the two brothers were brought back together again.

B: How do you know it was a film and not just an ordinary dream?

C: It just was!

[He looks at me as if to say 'can't you see it?' and I begin to think I am participating in a film pitch.]

B: Well, it's a cracking idea for a film!

Within this idea, he encapsulated a great deal of knowledge of film. He knew that films have to have key characters who have relationships with each other. He recognised the importance of dramatic moments which are sometimes connected to extreme weather (the storm) or to significant life events (a birthday). He also knew that films have to have a disruptive event early in the narrative: the dad's death and the brothers' separation. Finally, he showed that he understood the conventional requirement for resolution: the reuniting of the two brothers. What's more, he saw his idea in scenes, including flashback and flash forward, signalling his understanding of the way film can re-order time. He demonstrated a complex understanding of the underlying structures of narrative and the distinctive ways in which films tell stories.

It would be natural to assume that Connor's love of stories in the moving-image form could assist him in accessing the literacy curriculum. But he regularly said he was not good at writing and occasionally expressed frustration about the stories he had in his head that he thought should be turned into films. He was not motivated by getting his ideas down on paper because his writing failed to match up with his multimodal imaginings. Although his engagement with film enabled him to infer meaning and respond to audio-visual texts in complex ways, writing stories presented more difficulty:

> Well mainly people just start with once upon a time but I think that's a bit boring really. It's what you'd use in a fairytale really. I'd start with something like – say it's like in a film – in an actual film it's come up with all't writing. And then I'd like think – 'cos in some films it says the film name and then something like, someone could wake up really fast and then say, 'Oh we're late' or something like that. And then you think, 'Oh what are they late for?' And then that makes it into a mystery. But I'm not that good at writing. I can think of a story in my head. I can think it through but then I'm quite slow at writing.

This sounds rather like the opening scene of *Four Weddings and a Funeral* (dir. Newell, UK 1994), which Connor might well have seen. He was able to both read and then articulate explicitly the importance of setting up a question in the mind of the audience: what are they late for? This implies a sophisticated understanding of the relationship between audience, text and producer. However, Connor struggled to transfer this understanding to his writing. As an educator, this presented me with a dilemma about whether to accept that his ideas were moving-image-based and give him the opportunity to use film to tell stories, or whether to attempt to enable him to transform his filmic ideas into the written word. Kress (1995) argues that:

> The means for making representations which we provide for children and for adults, are the means which enable them to be fully human and fully social. (p. 75)

By limiting Connor's opportunities to draw on film in his own storytelling, we would limit his opportunity to be 'fully human and fully social'. By contrasting Connor's written work with his oral storytelling, I began to explore the impact of valuing what he already knew about stories from popular culture, and of offering him a range of modes of expression.

Teaching about story: current practice

When asked what makes a good story, all the children in the research group, except Connor, quickly began to talk about good writing. They used vocabulary and ideas from contemporary curriculum documents about teaching writing, particularly Ros Wilson's 'Big Writing' programme (2002), as passed down to them by teachers. Thus they described being given 'success criteria' in Year 4; they referred to punctuation, wow words, rainbow writing (if you use good words, you can't use them twice), speech, exclamation marks, connectives and power openers – terms they had learnt at school as being the key to reaching higher levels in their writing. Connor was the only one in the research group who did not mention what he had been taught about story in school. He answered the question entirely differently, saying: 'It depends on what sorts of stories you like.' It was noticeable that, unlike his peers, he did not insert into his writing awkward or ill-suited figurative language, overly formal openings or inappropriate connectives. He did, however, attempt to draw on the experiences of narrative he had gained from popular culture.

Myths and legends

The first substantial writing task the class undertook was to write the beginning of a Greek myth. Connor wrote:

Zenda and the legend of the wind waker

Long, long ago was a boy called Link and he had golden, shiny hair and he was known to be the legend of warriors. The evil gorgon had the power of strength and Link has the power of bravery and the power of wisdom.

[Loysin] the hands of Zelda. So the journey begins on lagoon island where his grandma lives. His grandma says to go and find his sister.

Link is the name of the main character in the popular musical film *Hairspray* (dir. Shankman, USA 2007), and a heroic character in

Nintendo's video-game series *The Legend of Zelda*: Connor appeared to be drawing on both. His choice of language to express the qualities of characters also reflected an influence from games. His use of the phrases 'the power of strength', 'the power of bravery' and 'the power of wisdom' recalled the attributes which game characters use to defeat others and make progress. Repetition and the use of 'so', 'long ago', 'so the journey begins' and 'long, long ago' imply a past fictional world with myths which the reader must navigate. However, Connor's account is more like the brief written back-story offered to introduce new game elements. The structure reflects the conventions of a traditional story: a happy status quo into which an enemy causes a disruption or conflict, so that we expect the hero to be involved in rescue or battle to overcome evil. This traditional story structure is also found in many quest games. But Connor did not draw on any visual or audio aspect of the game-world style. Neither did he use a first-person narrator, which might be expected since game players often participate as a character in the fictional world. He simply adopted the verbal style and language of game back-stories to indicate the generic features of his myth.

In their studies of how children's playing of online and computer games relates to their writing, Mackey (2004) and Bearne and Wolstencroft (2006) demonstrate the importance of the modal affordances of different texts. When children attempt to draw on a fairy story in order to create a game, they use both as resources, but it is the mode of the final outcome that determines the extent to which they can deploy their knowledge of games. In Bearne and Wolstencroft's study, the children were creating (paper-based) computer games which allowed them to express their knowledge of the conventions, structure and vocabulary of games in their own stories. In order for children to fully draw upon their knowledge of games, children need opportunities to create games, but they also need support to transfer their understandings of narrative, beyond structure and language, from games into their writing.

Animated films and comic strips

In his writing, Connor paid little attention to what Genette (1980) describes as discourse – that is to say, how stories are told. But in an oral storytelling game, he did become focused on description rather than narrative structure. The story began, 'Once upon a time there was a princess who lived in a magical kingdom with her cat':

And the cat turned into a big werewolf. And its claws snapped off and then big claws went 'shhhw' [demonstrates growth of claws by cat/wolf with hands]. And it turned into a werewolf and all its, all its. It walked into the shower so its skin went down, er its fur went down again so it wasn't all spikey. And when it came out it went like that [gestures cat/wolf shaking itself] and went all spikey again and then it went to look for the princess and it found a pea and it ate a pea and it got poisoned [Looks up to finish and passes story on].

What Connor described here was something he could see and hear as he described it. His description drew on animations such as *Tom and Jerry* (Hanna-Barbera, Dietch et al., MGM from 1940) or the more recent pastiche 'Itchy and Scratchy Show' which features on *The Simpsons* (Groening, C20 Fox TV from 1989). Benign paws turn suddenly into sharp claws. Fur sticks up and then appears smooth again. Using fur to express a wide range of meanings is a convention of cartoons and comic strips featuring animal characters. Spiked-up fur that makes a character look cool, scary or strong contrasts with flat fur that makes a character look silly. In his oral storytelling, Connor was able to pay more attention to this aspect of the discourse and in doing so drew on his understanding of drawn characters in cartoons and comic strips.

Connor introduced to this story the idea that characters can be flattened, exploded, poisoned and still 'live to see another day'. In this oral context, all the children were less concerned with rules, and became more playful. A wider range of characters appeared from popular culture including vampires, zombies and Star Wars protagonists. These new characters tended to be more dangerous and action-oriented than those in their school-based writing. Despite this more playful and transgressive approach to storytelling elicited by the use of spoken stories based on animated films, the children were concerned about coherence and paid far more attention to discourse because they were keen to take the audience with them in their storytelling. Clearly, medium and audience dramatically influence the extent to which the children participate in creating narrative.

Film-making

Connor was the only child in the group who had tried out film-making before the research started, at home. He had borrowed his gran's phone to experiment with a stop-motion animation technique, using voice-over and editing in camera. When it came to devising a storyline for his film, he already knew what he wanted to make. His idea was clearly influenced by his interest in street dance and talent-spotting reality TV shows.

During the script development period, Connor resisted writing anything down but he did add to and change his ideas as he started to see, in his mind, what would work on film. Parker (2006) found that, for some children, their film productions demonstrated their understanding of narrative far more effectively than their writing. This was certainly the case for Connor, whose story had a strong narrative arc from the first moment he thought of it. His six-minute film told the story of two friends who entered a talent contest to do street dance but fell out because of the competition between them. The story also featured a headmaster who wanted his own favourite pupil, a ballet dancer, to win. The story ended with the boys consolidating their friendship and jointly winning the competition. Connor's film scenario had a far more complex narrative structure than he had achieved in his writing, having not only a main but also a secondary storyline.

Many moments in the process of production, including scripting, casting, shooting, acting, editing and selecting the soundtrack, indicated that Connor was highly engaged by the process and keen to ensure the final film was as close as it could be to how he imagined it. For example, in storyboarding his script, something he was not enthusiastic about doing, Connor drew everything in long shot. When it came to filming, even of scenes he appeared in and therefore couldn't shoot himself, he took the lead in determining where the camera should be positioned. He soon realised that in some cases a long shot would not have the impact he wanted, so he changed to close-up in order to ensure the audience could see the emotions in the two boys' faces. Throughout the process, Connor showed an acute awareness of the potential impact of the film story on its audience. This skill is highly prized when found in children's writing but in Connor's writing it was distinctly absent. His writing often did not take the reader with him. He assumed the audience had knowledge of the scenario in his head. What he missed out were the things the audience would be able to see, hear and infer if watching the story as a moving image. This is shown by Connor's attempt to put the story of his film into writing:

Step to the Challenge

One day there was a couple of kids speaking to each other on the school yard. One kid called Zak (the big show off) and all the others we don't need to discuss anyway. Another kid called Joe (Zak's best friend) was walking up to Zak.

Joe: Hay Zak what's up?

Zak: Have you heard about the talent competition, I'm so going to win

Joe: Can I enter?

Zak: Yea but it costs £1 to enter

So he entered. The next day the competition started Joe was first

Joe: I was ok I got two yeses and one no

Zak: My turn

When finished he came out and said,

Zak: Did you see that I was wicked

Joe: Stop bragging you loser

The next day Zak was up against Joe in the challenge

Zak: You may as well just give up, Joe

Joe: What and back down from a loser like you. No way

Millard (1997) suggests that the way films are edited, which she interprets primarily as a process of shot juxtaposition, influences children's writing, making it 'jerky' and overly reliant on dialogue. But on the strength of research that compares children's creative work in film-making and in writing, Parker (2001) argues that the actual experience of film-making may encourage empathy in descriptive writing, and greater attention to contextual factors such as time, space and causality. So the problems identified by Millard might be addressed through a closer attention to film.

Both in films and in written texts, a range of different creative choices are available, governing what needs to be told/shown, and what can be implied. Children do not 'naturally' understand this. They can unconsciously understand how character and plot interrelate, and they can work intertextually, drawing on a wide range of sources in their writing and other storytelling forms. But they don't necessarily understand explicitly how these forms work as discourses. As a consequence, they tend to focus just on plot or characters, leaving gaps in their writing which, in films, games and cartoons, would be filled by the use of visual, audio and spatial elements, comprehensible to an audience that instinctively recognises the conventions of film-making. So media teaching in the primary classroom needs to make space for reflecting on the different ways in which filmed and written texts make meaning. It is not enough simply to use films as a stimulus for writing.

Some key differences between these two modes can be understood if we consider how each manages time. In film, it is editing that shows the temporal relationship between events, and builds expectations about what will happen next. So, for example, when a character leaves a room, a shot of a closing door, or perhaps just the sound of slamming, might signal their exit, and one or more reaction shots of the characters left behind can indicate the significance of this departure. We do not need to see the full sequence of the character getting up, walking across the floor and opening and shutting the door in order to be able to make the appropriate inferences. In a written text, the addition of descriptive words and phrases (such as 'suddenly', 'swiftly', 'angrily', 'slamming the door') elaborates the basic information 'he left the room' by adding temporal and emotional 'markers'.

In the written version of his film story, Connor does explicitly tell the reader not to pay attention to the 'other' characters, but he lacks a range of other devices for signalling what they ought to pay attention to. He omits descriptive terms and although there is a sequence of events, he does not attempt to use any language beyond simple temporal and spatial measures ('one day', 'on the school yard', 'the next day') to create transitions between one scene and the next, despite having done this successfully in his film.

The notion of the storyteller's power to include or withhold aspects of the story became a preoccupation for Connor through the course of the research process. He started to see storytelling as a trail of clues, but he did not learn how to make the transition from filmic to written conventions for constructing and laying clues. As a result, all his knowledge and experiences of storytelling were undervalued, with dramatic consequences. At my last visit to the school, Connor had become a regular absentee, increasingly disengaged from school life.

Conclusion

It is important to acknowledge that the influence of film and other aspects of popular culture enrich children's 'funds of knowledge' (Moll et al., 1992) of the narrative form, and that recognising and valuing them in schools may be the first stage of a longer process of enabling them to draw on them usefully in their writing. This includes enabling children to express stories in a range of forms including films, games, comics and cartoons. They do, however, need further support when transforming their experiences of non-print narrative into written stories. Reid (2003) argues that film can be used to scaffold writing and that children can learn about narrative by 'shuttling' between film and print in order to engage with the different modes of each form: to understand what they have in common and what is specific to each form. It became evident that in order for Connor to become a motivated and curious learner and to be able to demonstrate his 'fund of knowledge' about stories, he needed not only to be invited to draw on his particular love and rich repertoire of films, cartoons and games, but also to be encouraged to reflect upon the differences as well as the similarities between filmed and written texts.

References

Barrs, M. (2004) 'The reader in the writer', in T. Grainger (ed.) *Reader in Language and Literacy*. London and New York: RoutledgeFalmer, pp. 267–76.

Bearne, E. and Wolstencroft, H. (2006) 'Playing with texts: the contribution of children's knowledge of computer narratives to their story-writing', in J. Marsh and E. Millard (eds) *Popular Literacies, Childhood and Schooling*. London and New York: Routledge, pp. 72–92.

Genette, G. (1980) (trans. J.E. Lewin) *Narrative Discourse: An Essay on Method*. Ithaca, NY: Cornell University Press.

Giddens, A. (1991) *Modernity and Self Identity: Self and Society in the Late Modern Age*. Cambridge: Polity Press.

Kress, G. (1995) *Writing the Future: English and the Making of a Culture of Innovation*. Sheffield: National Association for the Teaching of English (NATE).

Mackey, M. (2004) *Literacies across Media: Playing the Text*. London: Routledge/Falmer Revised edition, 2007. Final chapter reprinted in *The Routledge/Falmer Reader in Language and Literacy*, T. Grainger (ed.). London: Routledge/Falmer, 2004.

Millard, E. (1997) *Differently Literate: Boys, Girls and the Schooling of Literacy*. London and Washington, DC: Falmer Press.

Moll, L.C., Armanti, C., Neff, D. and Gonzalez, N. (1992) 'Funds of knowledge for teaching: using a qualitative approach to connect homes and classrooms', *Theory into Practice*, 31 (2): 132–41.

Parker, D. (2001) *Moving Image, Media, Print Literacy and Narrative*. Available at www.bfi.org.uk/education/research/teachlearn/nate.html (retrieved 30 December 2009).

Parker, D. (2006) 'Making it move, making it mean: animation, print literacy and the metafunctions of language', in J. Marsh and E. Millard (eds) *Popular Literacies, Childhood and Schooling*. London: Routledge Falmer.

Reid, M. (2003) 'Writing film: making inferences when viewing and reading', *Reading*, 37 (3): 111–15.

Wilson, R. (2002) *Raising Standards in Writing*. Kirklees Council: School Effectiveness Service.

Points for Practice

Film Adaptations

Cary Bazalgette

The aim of this activity is to encourage children to reflect on the differences between the ways in which films (and also games and graphic novels) can make meaning, and the ways in which meanings can be created in writing.

Play a minute or so of the soundtrack of a film, preferably one that they are unlikely to know (see 'Finding Films to Watch', page 46), and preferably a soundtrack that includes plenty of interesting sound effects, not just music or dialogue – although you can also do this activity just with a piece of music.

Ask the children to listen carefully to the soundtrack several times. You could divide the class into groups, and give each a specific listening task – for example:

1. Listen for sounds that suggest what time of day it is.
2. Listen for sounds that may indicate something about a character (note that a character is not necessarily a person!).
3. Listen for sounds that may indicate something about a place.
4. Listen for sounds that may suggest what is going to happen in the story.

After the children have reported back on what they have heard (this is likely to set up several different possibilities), you can show them the film extract and they can discuss the similarities and differences between their interpretations of the soundtrack and their interpretations of the film extract itself. This should highlight the constructed nature of film: that the soundtrack and the visuals work together to make meaning.

Now – finally – ask the children to write one sentence each that starts to tell the story they have been watching. These can be read out or displayed, and discussed. The aim is not to come up with 'good' pieces of writing, but to highlight the different choices that the children will have made, for example:

- whether to use first- or third-person narration
- whether to use the present or past tense
- whether to start with a detail or by setting the whole scene
- whether to use a temporal marker, e.g. 'one day' or 'once upon a time'
- whether to name a character and provide a description of them.

None of these is a 'right' or 'wrong' choice: the important outcome of the activity is for children to reflect upon the differences between filmed and written stories in terms of the creative choices that are open to film-makers and to writers. It may also be possible to reflect upon the kinds of things that are difficult to film but easy to write, and vice versa.

These approaches are based on ideas in the BFI resources *Story Shorts 2* and *Starting Stories 2* (see www.bfi.org.uk/education/teaching/primary.html).

Points for Practice

Book Adaptations

Geraldine Walker

The aim here is to sharpen children's realisation that films and books tell stories in different ways. Although both are constructed, and there are some similarities between them, they use distinctive modes of expression in order to make meaning and tell stories, and can include and omit different things. The aim is not to show that one is better than the other, but to explore the differences and similarities between the two modes.

Any book which has been made into a film can be used for this activity – one of the Harry Potter books and films might be an obvious choice. There are websites where you can download screenplays (for example, www.simply scripts.com) so if there is not one available for the book adaptation you are working on, you can download an example and use it as a template.

Photocopy the opening of the story from the book and, depending on the level of the pupils, decide on the length of text to read. For this exercise, it is better to keep the text quite short: it might just be a few sentences.

Ask them to highlight all the sentences/phrases which can be made into an image and then ask each child or pair to choose one for which they want to draw the images.

Look at the sentences/phrases not highlighted and discuss why these cannot be used in a visual way. This can be developed by highlighting adjectives/adverbs.

Share the images they have drawn, on a wall display or projected on the IWB. Could these be used to create an opening sequence of the film, and if so in what order?

What words, sounds or music would they need to add to these images to make sure they would be understood?

Download a copy of the screenplay if possible. Look at the information which is included in a script. What are the major differences between the descriptions in the book and the information in the screenplay?

Now watch the opening sequence of the film and discuss the differences between the text from the book, their planning and the screenplay.

Social Media and Primary School Children

Guy Merchant

Chapter objectives

This chapter describes some new social media applications and argues for their value in the classroom, using the concept of 'transmedia' to identify and summarise an important repertoire of skills for drawing on different kinds of text in the construction of meaning. Six specific issues about the classroom use of social media are addressed in order to support planning for this kind of activity.

It's a rainy morning in November and Hannah is putting the finishing touches to a storyboard for her Animoto presentation on Neptune. She's already sourced some stock images and some movie footage, and Rob her class teacher has shown her group how short captions, still and moving images combine with music to good effect on Animoto. Hannah's short presentation will be posted on a blog shared between six other primary schools in the city. She hopes to receive plenty of comments as feedback and is eager to see what the other nine-year-olds have been up to. After school that day she sends a message from home to her friends asking how it went for the other groups in her class who have each chosen different projects as part of Rob's *Earth and Space* theme.

These children's use of Animoto, an online environment that allows you to upload and sequence images and then set them to music, builds on both their home experience of media and their school-based work over several years. The finished projects will be shared online, and children from a network of schools in the area will view and comment on the work. In their previous year, the children in Rob's class used a similar application called Voicethread to present their history work to other schools. Like Animoto, Voicethread enables users to share images, documents and media online. In Voicethread, these media can be sequenced and synchronised with an audio commentary. The presentation is then displayed in the centre of the screen. Visitors to a particular Voicethread can record comments using various media, and these are displayed around the edge of the presentation. So the final Voicethread becomes an amalgam of the original presentation and the feedback received. In exploring the theme of *The Romans*, the children created quizzes in PowerPoint, information leaflets in Word, and even a movie interview with a Roman citizen – played by a classmate dressed in a toga made from a bedsheet. These Voicethreads received many enthusiastic comments from children in partner schools.

School systems are often criticised for their inherently conservative nature, and teachers for their resistance to change. Furthermore, classrooms in much of the English-speaking world have, for the last 10 years or so, been dominated by a 'back-to-basics' agenda with a strong emphasis on the skills associated with traditional print literacy (Carrington, 2009). Not, one might think, a particularly fertile ground for development work on new media. But teachers like Rob do exist, and are an inspiration because they quietly continue to provide children with a rich experience of school – one that values their knowledge and takes advantage of new forms of communication. In planning his work around *Earth and Space*, Rob observes to me that the recommended curriculum is 'a bit boring'. He is keen to help children to build meanings together, under his guidance. Working with what some describe as Web 2.0 applications (Di Nucci, 1999) like Animoto and Voicethread, is important to him in promoting the ethos of 'social media', both in and beyond his classroom. In social media, meanings are produced collectively and shared democratically, rather than being 'handed down' from a single source.

The examples of practice from Rob's school are indicative of the participatory learning often associated with the use of Web 2.0 in the classroom (Davies and Merchant, 2009). Although not entirely unproblematic, this kind of work has some significant positive features. First, it seems that pupils are highly motivated – partly because they can draw on familiar formats (such as the TV-style interview of the Roman citizen, mentioned above) and partly because their work is stored for successive viewings. Second, classroom work becomes more widely available – to friends and relatives as well as to pupils in other schools. And, third, because of the socially interactive dimension, visitors to the sites can leave comments, provide feedback and enrich the original presentation. Social media applications like Animoto and Voicethread are attractive because they are accessible to most users, in the sense that they don't assume a high level of technical expertise. For instance, in Rob's class, minor technical problems are usually solved by the children without the need for any intervention by him.

Rob's classroom contains a wall display that showcases the children's work on film narrative, covering some details of their work on editing and camera angles, but what is more interesting about the social media the children are using is the wide variety of skills and understanding required. Some of these build on their work on film narrative, whereas others seem quite distinct. The Animoto composition process enables some similarities but also some differences between this work and more conventional digital video editing. Animoto and Voicethread provide opportunities for relatively short, interactive presentations and involve what some of us working in the field have begun to describe as 'transmedia skills'. Where moving image is incorporated, it is more likely to be in the short form more commonly associated with YouTube than with cinema; where a text document is included, an economy of words is preferable; and the soundtrack (or voice commentary) becomes a key cohesive device. These and other aspects may help to suggest how social media can be different from established media, but they also make thinking critically about social media even more important. In what follows, I begin by addressing the issue of learning in social media. This is followed by a section on selecting social media for the classroom. I conclude by looking at how we might apply some of the principles of media literacy to this sort of work.

What are we learning today?

When we reflect on the sort of practices described above, it soon becomes clear that existing models of description are called into question.

We might well ask, what exactly are the children engaged in? Certainly, neither the teacher nor his class would describe the work they were doing as 'media education', let alone something as unfamiliar as an education in 'social media'. The core purposes of the activities described are to involve and present children's learning in interesting ways, using the benefits that new technology offers. Engaging with curriculum, learning itself and looking for ways of presenting new understandings, are central concerns here. In fact, media work is occupying the same sort of space that literacy once did in the 'literacy across the curriculum' movement – it becomes a space for making and sharing meanings. In doing so, however, it is not simply a hand-maiden for the wider curriculum, because there is also a clear set of understandings and skills underpinning it.

The idea of *transmedia* is useful here in trying to unpick what lies behind these emerging practices. To start with, it may be worth first tracing the origins of the term. In an influential book, Kinder (1991) uses the term 'transmedia intertextuality' to describe the distribution of material objects from different media that feed off each other to create meanings. This is seen, for example, in the way that a new film is often marketed alongside its soundtrack, an accompanying video game, clothing and other product tie-ins.

The transmedia concept has been taken up by educators such as Dyson (2001) and Marsh (2005). Dyson explores the ways in which popular narratives from TV programmes, video games, books and magazines are woven into children's writing in the classroom. The focus of Dyson's work is on the way in which these media narratives are re-fashioned when children compose through writing and drawing. But the idea of transmedia work could also be used to describe the composition of texts *in* different media. This is what Qian alludes to when she argues that:

> ... one of the major goals of new media literacy education in the digital age is to develop students' transmedia skills. Students' technical and literacy skills across multiple media channels and modalities become especially important in this technology-rich and media-saturated learning environment ... Equally important ... are the spirit, habit, and skills of inquiry. (2009: 267)

What is of significance here is not only the idea of developing technical skills across media, important though this may be, but the suggestion that more generic attitudes of mind and dispositions towards learning are involved. This might, for instance, encompass the learning that emerges from what Graham (2008) calls the 'playfully social', the ways in which learners could benefit from network effects, or the early stages of a sort of interest-driven collective intelligence in which knowledge is produced and distributed collaboratively (Gee, 2004).

An indication of the transmedia work involved in producing an Animoto presentation can be usefully illustrated by Hannah's plan of her work on Neptune (Figure 8.1). Using the familiar storyboard format – a sheet of A4 is folded three times to create eight frames – she produces a plan that suggests both the ideational and the presentational aspects of the work.

Although not always explicit about the detail, the plan indicates an introductory title and countdown soundtrack, video and still image material, and short items of informational commentary. Her intention is that these elements will work together to present her learning to others. Collation of the factual detail about Neptune, which relates to the class's Earth and Space topic, actually takes place alongside the compositional skills. She indicates in the plan how informational content will be distributed across time, and how image, sound and written text might be orchestrated in the Animoto presentation. Although, at one level, these might be considered as generic skills for working with moving images, the short form and the specific affordances of the software seem to work together to suggest a distinct genre. And this in turn makes it difficult to judge what makes a 'good' Animoto presentation, and where teachers might position such work on the broader map of experience in media. Even if we put aside criticisms of the storyboard approach (see, for instance, Buckingham, 2003: 133), we are still left with the familiar concern: what constitutes progression in media work?

But this is not the only issue. Accepting the point made above about attitudes of mind and dispositions to learning is to acknowledge that Hannah's work is produced in the expectation that it will be shared and commented on by others outside her immediate school context – co-learners with whom she may not have a face-to-face relationship. Audience feedback and evaluation of her work will be an important part of her learning. Seen like this, the Neptune presentation is less like a short film and more like a YouTube video, for which the number and nature of the comments received are viewed as a marker of success (Davies and Merchant, 2009). This in turn raises questions about the role and nature of feedback. Will the audience react to the aesthetic appeal of her presentation or to what they

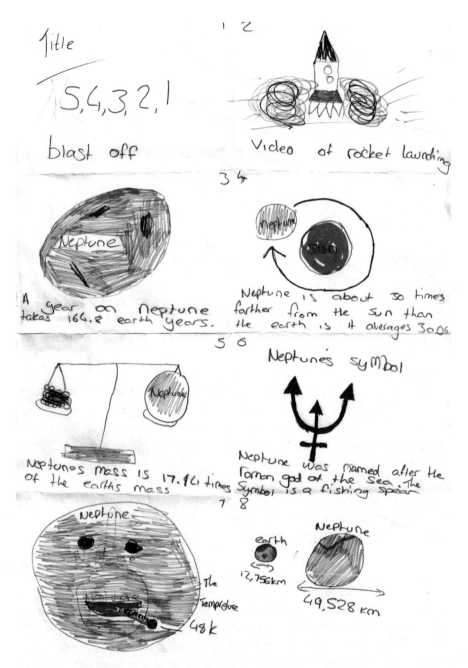

Figure 8.1 Hannah's Animoto plan

learn about Neptune – or both? And does it matter? Furthermore, because this work takes place in an educational context, to what extent should teachers be guiding or encouraging particular sorts of comments?

Considering this work from what I have called a transmedia perspective raises some significant questions – questions to which, I suspect, there are no easy answers. Yet it does seem important that children are given structured experiences of producing work that use these skills, involving, as they do, some basic and generalisable ways of thinking, as well as fulfilling the function of connecting learners to audiences beyond the classroom. Perhaps also the work outlined plays to the strengths of social media and suggests its wider role in learning. It is unlikely that making an Animoto presentation constitutes a skill for life, but it certainly does involve worthwhile creative processes that constitute a good introduction to social media.

Social media in the classroom

Although so far, for illustrative purposes, I have focused on one piece of work and one particular application, fluidity in the development of Web 2.0 tools poses problems for professional commentary since very often, by the time of publication, the tool may be unavailable or may have the changed functionality associated with a later version. At the time of writing, there is plenty of evidence of educators experimenting with sites like Cooliris, Voicethread, Bubbleshare and Glogster, but there is no telling whether these sites will still be around in their present form as you read this. Nonetheless it seems possible to begin to identify and articulate the underlying issues around using social media in the classroom, as well as to raise some more practical questions that, as educators, we need to explore. I conclude with some issues that teachers should consider when planning to use social media in the classroom. These can be framed as six key questions:

1. What kinds of learning are intended?

The example of Rob's Earth and Space topic provides us with an interesting way in to this issue. Researching and presenting factual information about the planets was clearly the main purpose for his work; but he also has a clear understanding of the benefits of social media. However, one could imagine how the use of presentational tools could depend more explicitly on the aesthetic impact or media capabilities involved. Children could, for example, be asked to draw up evaluative criteria and assess the piece in terms of its effectiveness; or comparisons might be made between two or more social media.

What, for instance, are the advantages and disadvantages of creating a Glogster multimedia poster as opposed to an Animoto presentation?

2. What sort of understandings does the social media site assume?

Teachers of primary-age children need to be familiar with the range of social media sites available if they are to make good use of them in the classroom. This, in itself, is a substantial challenge, partly because of the rapidly changing nature of social media, but also because it requires regular updating in a sector of the teaching profession quite understandably more often concerned with face-to-face work than anything else. CPD providers, technology specialists and local advisers have an important role to play here in evaluating, advocating, recommending and disseminating work that involves the use of social media. But this is no substitute for teachers' first-hand experience; they need time to investigate the tools themselves in order to gauge the understanding and skills necessary for participation. This is crucial in integrating this work into classroom practice.

3. What will need to be taught or explained before children get involved?

This follows quite naturally from the previous questions, but here the focus is on implementation. Teachers need to think through how social media can be embedded in practice. This will include a consideration of the transmedia skills involved, a view of the children's prior knowledge, anticipation of problems that might arise and identifying an audience for the work produced. The question of audience is particularly significant, because it is a key feature of social media. Although this aspect can be introduced *within* the school context by sharing work between classes, it really comes into its own when it is shared between schools or between home and school – and of course this introduces another layer of complication. Some of the most fruitful work to emerge so far has built on existing clusters of schools – schools usually located in a relatively small geographical area. This is partly because effective cross-school collaboration depends on shared understandings which are often built through face-to-face meetings between teachers. However, this is by no means a pre-requisite of social media work and certainly there are good examples of international collaborations (Merchant, 2009) in which teachers have coordinated activities through the use of social media.

4. How easy is it to access the site?

Access to social media sites is usually very straightforward, simply requiring an authentic email address, a username and a password. Most social media sites offer a basic service free of charge, and an enhanced service for a small fee. This enhanced service often allows a larger amount of content to be uploaded. For instance, in the case of Animoto, a pay account lets users make longer presentations. The next obstacle may be that school safety filters block access to some sites (see Davies and Merchant, 2009), so this warrants initial exploration. Third, not all schools provide children with individual email accounts. And, finally, as we probably all know, it is frustratingly easy to forget usernames and passwords! If there are ways around these four issues, then the use of social media sites can be reasonably straightforward. Teachers may then need to consider whether children should be encouraged to access the site from home, which itself would give rise to further issues.

5. How easy is it to register/set up accounts?

Although some of the basic issues have been addressed above, there are some further practical issues at the stage of registration – and these can be time-consuming. Some sites – particularly those aimed at the educational market – have recognised this and provide ways around it. So, for example, the wiki-farm PBworks (formerly PBwiki), allows teachers, as administrators, to enrol users without email addresses, while Voicethread provides a specific teacher log-in that enables multiple accounts to be activated. There is nothing more frustrating than planning to use social media, and generating pupil interest along the way, only to find that logging in is problematic and the verification process painfully slow. So it is certainly worth spending time in testing out the logistics of registration before introducing it to the children.

6. How can safety issues be addressed?

Although some measures taken by educators in the name of e-safety may inhibit educational uses of the internet by inadvertently blocking access to good sites (Davies and Merchant, 2009), teachers will want to be reassured that the use of social media will not expose children to risk. The difficulty here is that the default assumption in social media is that published material is open to all. Uploaded material is public in the widest sense. However, some sites allow viewing by invitation only (you can mark your material as private) and others allow you to moderate comments. Social media companies with an interest in the schools market have given some of these issues careful consideration. So, for example, Animoto's education interface explains how teachers of younger children can monitor activity by using dummy email addresses (there is a clear explanation of how to set these up), and how presentations remain private (Animoto, 2009).

Conclusion

Social media offer some new and exciting possibilities for educators. Perhaps the most interesting of these are opportunities for new or extended forms of participation and collaboration. Authors like Jenkins (2006) and Buckingham (2003) have explored the notion that new technologies can help to support new kinds of participation. In his writing on media, Jenkins regularly uses the term 'participatory culture' to capture this theme, suggesting the importance of audience engagement and collective intelligence in popular media. In an influential paper written for the MacArthur Foundation, a participatory culture is described as one in which members 'believe their contributions matter, and feel some degree of social connection with one another' (Jenkins et al., 2006: 3). It is argued that new communications technology has transformed the lives of many (but not all), and that transmedia skills are necessary for full participation in the digital world. There is, however, a 'participation gap'; therefore, these skills should, according to the MacArthur report, be incorporated in the school curriculum.

An alternative view and one that suggests a more reflective or critical producer and consumer comes from the European Charter for Media Literacy (2004). In contrast to Jenkins' model, the European Charter is more explicitly educational, describing its aims in terms of literacies, while at the same time underscoring the importance of criticality. The charter identifies three interrelated strands of learning, often referred to as the three Cs:

- Cultural: broadening learners' experience of different kinds of media form and content

- Critical: developing learners' critical skills in analysing and assessing media outputs

- Creative: developing learners' creative skills in using media for expression and communication, and for participation in public debate.

Although these strands are clearly open to interpretation, they do provide a perspective that can help us to examine work involving social media. So the use of tools like Animoto and Voicethread can provide a good introduction to the cultural and creative dimensions of media literacy. For me, and I suspect for teachers like Rob, developing the critical dimension is more problematic. Frameworks for reading media texts, such as those proposed by Buckingham (2003) and Burn and Parker (2003), provide a useful starting point for such work, but these now need to be applied to classroom practices such as those described in this chapter. If we are living in a world in which children and young people are becoming literate across media, and are regular participants in online environments, then there is clearly a need for more development work of the kind described in this chapter.

References

Animoto (2009) *Getting Started with Animoto for Education*. Available at http://animoto.com/education/getting_started (retrieved 12 October 2009).

Buckingham, D. (2003) *Media Education: Literacy, Learning and Contemporary Culture*. Cambridge: Polity Press.

Burn, A. and Parker, D. (2003) *Analysing Media Texts*. London: Continuum.

Carrington, V. (2009) 'From blog to bebo and beyond: text, risk, participation', *Journal of Research in Reading*, 32 (1): 6–22.

Davies, J. and Merchant, G. (2009) *Web 2.0 for Schools: Learning and Social Participation*. New York: Peter Lang.

Di Nucci, D. (1999) *Fragmented Future*. Available at www.cdinucci.com/Darcy2/articles/Print/Printarticle7.html (retrieved 3 January 2010).

Dyson, A.H. (2001) 'Donkey Kong in Little Bear Country: a first grader's composing development in the media spotlight,' *The Elementary School Journal*, 101 (4): 417–33.

Euromedia (2004) *European Charter for Media Literacy*. Available at www.euromedialiteracy.eu/charter.php (retrieved 16 October 2009).

Gee, J.P. (2004) *What Videogames Have to Teach us About Learning and Literacy*. New York: Palgrave Macmillan.

Graham, L. (2008) 'Teachers are digikids too: the digital histories and digital lives of young teachers in English primary schools', *Literacy*, 42 (1): 10–18.

Jenkins, H. (2006) *Fans, Bloggers and Gamers: Exploring Participatory Culture*. New York: New York University Press.

Jenkins, H. with Purushota, R., Clinton, K., Weigel, M. and Robinson, A. (2006) *Confronting the Challenges of Participatory Culture: Media Education for the 21st Century*. Chicago: MacArthur Foundation. Available at www.digitallearning.macfound.org/atf/cf/%7B7E45C7E0-A3E0-4B89-AC9C-E807E1B0AE4E%7D/JENKINS_WHITE_PAPER.PDF (retrieved 27 August 2009).

Kinder, M. (1991) *Playing with Power in Movies, Television, and Video Games*. Berkeley, CA: University of California Press.

Marsh, J. (2005) 'Ritual, performance and identity construction: young children's engagement with popular cultural and media texts', in J. Marsh (ed.) *Popular Culture, New Media and Digital Literacy in Early Childhood*. London: Routledge Falmer, pp. 28–55.

Merchant, G. (2009) 'Web 2.0, new literacies, and the idea of learning through participation', *English Teaching: Practice and Critique*, 8 (3): 8–20.

Qian, Y. (2009) 'New media literacy in 3-D virtual learning environments', in L. Hin and R. Subramaniam (eds) *Handbook of Research on New Media Literacy at the K-12 Level: Issues and Challenges*. New York: IGI Global, pp. 257–70.

Case Study 1

Alternate Reality in the Classroom

Angela Colvert

A mysterious email arrives and is read aloud by the teacher to the class of 8- and 9-year-olds. It's from two secret agents, Onyx and Violet Linton. In it they explain that there's a beast on the loose and that they are in desperate need of help! After an initial explanation as to why their class has been selected, the children decide to investigate the web address included in the email. They find out about a place called Ocean Estate and its inhabitants in their search for more information relating to this strange creature. As the week goes on, the children's ideas develop as more information is revealed, distributed over a wide range of modes and media. The people of Ocean Estate post webcam diaries, write and respond to messages on the community forums and can be contacted by telephone. In order to solve the mystery, the class discusses the importance of the information with each other, with Onyx and Violet and the residents of Ocean Estate both online and offline. They decide on the next steps: the questions that need to be answered and elements that need further investigation. They couldn't solve the mystery without the help of these strangers, but they must act with caution. When contacted, the residents respond, and when asked, they are even prepared to send special artefacts through the post: maps, books, even 'potion ingredients'. As the class collates and interprets the information, a plan emerges: they must act quickly if the monster is to be captured …

This adventure was an alternate reality game (ARG) designed for the class by an inventive class of 10- and 11-year-olds in the same school. It was based on the novel *Mighty Fizz Chilla* by Philip Ridley (2002) and was created in response to the challenges of bringing the story to life for their peers. These older children were hidden behind the scenes during play, writing and acting in role as the characters from Ocean Estate and, prior to play, the children had spent most of the school year designing the experience and making the necessary game elements: films, websites, artefacts, etc. This exciting cross-curricular project, which met the requirements of the National Curriculum, was developed in discussion with the children, who contributed to its content and the pedagogic construction.

(Continued)

(Continued)

They shared their understandings, expertise and ideas in discussion with others in the class both online and offline, and used the same communication technologies to plan and design the game as were later used to play it.

The older children wanted the texts they produced to appear authentic and believable and didn't want to reveal themselves to the younger class as the creators of the game until the concluding moments of the experience. They experimented with the affordances and communicative potential of the modes and media at their disposal and, in so doing, demonstrated and developed a sophisticated understanding of the media practices and texts with which they engage.

Digital Glue: Creative Media in the Classroom

Tim Brook

Chapter objectives

This chapter describes the attractions and the disadvantages of animation, live action and digital storytelling as creative options before focusing on puppetry as the most appropriate technique for classroom film-making. Five phases of the production process are described in practical detail.

Why make movies?

Matthew came in early. He was slightly anxious because his mum had lent him her camera to use in the project we were going to be working on. He wanted to know how to get the pictures and video from the camera to the computer. I showed him and he went away happy. Later in the morning, while his teacher and I drew breath, she asked if I had seen his work. I replied, truthfully, that I thought he was doing an excellent job. 'I know!' she said enthusiastically, 'and he's really not very bright you know …' Then we looked at each other in the significant way teachers do as we both slowly absorbed the meanings of what she had just said. My conclusion was that he, and many like him, have insufficient opportunities to demonstrate or develop their ability for making meaning, outside the spoken or written systems that school so often prescribes.

Any teacher of film-making with children will quickly observe the richness and depth of their children's learning and the delight children take in that learning. Film-making requires the practice of skills detailed in the arts curriculum, with many others from English and communications. The content, however, can be drawn from any curricular area. So children might use images of Henry VIII's wives to create a biopic, or animated stick figure software to give a guided tour of the digestive system.

Management

The issues that are most likely to prevent you from making films with your children are your lack of skills, time and money. These problems can be circumvented, but you need to plan carefully in advance and make some realistic choices about what you can undertake, always bearing in mind that it is best to keep things as simple and modest as you can. This chapter assumes that you are embarking upon film-making with a whole class, and for the first time. It also assumes that film-making is not something that you and your class will just do once, but is something that you will want to offer to children on a regular basis all through the year, so that their film-making skills can develop and grow.

It sounds obvious but remember: the shorter your film is to be, the less time it will take to make. The simple approach I outline below requires a spoken narrative. One minute of continuous spoken narrative will require about 100 words of text. For your first production, or when time presses, aim for one to two minutes.

Dividing the project into sections and giving the sections to 'crews' to produce from start to finish rarely allows time for much hanging around. If you wish, you can assign studio roles to each member of your crews:

- Director – the one everybody will listen to with respect; has to be good at seeing the big picture

- Producer – the well-organised (slightly bossy) one

- Cinematographer – someone good at looking carefully

- Sound Engineer – someone good at listening carefully

- Art Director – someone who can draw their ideas (and probably doodles a lot)

- Editor – a computer-literate perfectionist.

To ensure that everyone is occupied, it is always a good idea to have some film-related activities available. Making film posters, tickets, sticker badges or invitations to the premiere will all enrich the project and keep children busy in slack moments. Most of the time, however, it will be 'all hands to the pump'. Publishing and using a schedule that details the tasks to be completed and their deadlines, keeps you and the children on track. Everyone needs to know the meaning of 'good enough'. Obviously, if more time is available, that will reduce the panic and probably improve the quality of production too. If it is the first time you have done anything like this, you should certainly allow longer and be prepared for the unexpected. But, with a little practice, you can easily make a short film in a day – and a very short one in less. However, you need to decide what kind of film to make. There are four possibilities.

Animation is popular with children and teachers – often because of the undoubted wow-factor of making models, Plasticine, paper cut-outs or drawings come to life. This said, something that has a great wow-factor for the makers does not always convey itself to a critical audience. When animating, it is all too easy for children to focus on the objects to be animated rather than on how they function as tools for communicating ideas. In making a 'claymation' movie (Plasticine model animation), for example, this might mean that the aesthetics and technicalities of model making dominate, with a disproportionate amount of time being spent on making good-looking but clumsy models that are difficult to move. For novices, it is essential to have a clear storyboard detailing the type of shot and the camera angle; even the most beautifully made and animated models will become boring with a continuous single frame and angle, as well as wasting an opportunity to explore the visual grammar of film.

A reasonable-quality animation rate is 15 frames per second (fps). That means a one-minute film will require 900 frames to be captured.

In each of those frames, a tiny movement is needed and children are often tempted to speed things up by increasing the size of movement. With young children, it can often be better to accept this and capture movement at fewer fps, or capture multiple copies of each frame and dispense with an attempt at smooth or realistic movement. The uncomplicated nature of Peter Firmin's stop-go animation mattered little when combined with his delightful artwork and Oliver Postgate's incomparable storytelling. Watch any of them via www.oliverpostgate.co.uk for inspiration.

Essential items are a tripod for claymation or models and some kind of rostrum for 2D animation. If you are using a Digi Blue camera, fix the stand down with plenty of Blu-Tack; and a boom microphone stand will serve as a rostrum.

Live action films in school *sound* like a straightforward idea: just point the camera at the performers and press 'record'. There are however many hidden complications.

Action sequences require especially careful planning to be convincing. Most children (and many adults) think it's fine to follow action with the camera in a continuous movement – a practice known disparagingly among professionals as 'hosepiping'. Watch how film-makers use their cameras. Most film is a series of shots (rarely more than 10 seconds) using a range of angles and proximities to make meaning. This requires careful planning – or a great deal of editing.

Realistically, you are probably limited to working within the confines of school. Your sick room might double up as a bedroom and your staff room as a kitchen or sitting room. It's pretty tricky to create a mediaeval village, the surface of the moon or a rainforest though. Also, you can almost guarantee it will rain on the day you are planning to shoot in the school grounds. Judicious use of footage filmed outside school can be added in to widen the apparent horizons; and using a close-up can disguise the location you are filming in. Careful placing of children between a digital projector and screen allows for the filming of shadow performances in exotic locations.

Children will need to learn lines and will forget them too – usually at the end of an otherwise perfect take. Your lead performer will suddenly be away for a week. One way of getting round such problems is by using face masks and separately recorded sound. Another advantage of using masks is that you can have several different children playing one part; and shy performers can suddenly become outrageous extroverts when wearing a mask. And, of course, the children are impossible to recognise unless you know them already – making it safe to display your movie online.

Digital stories are short, often personal stories that use a combination of voice, still images, text and occasionally short video clips. Using still images allows for a combination of sources, including specially taken photographs, scanned photographs or artwork, digital artwork and 'found' images. These images can be brought to life using the pan-and-zoom 'rostrum camera' effects available in video software packages such as Windows Movie Maker (available on most PCs) or separate free download packages like Photo Story (see also Chapter 8). It is far simpler for an individual or pairs to create digital stories than it is to shoot on video from scratch. Also, it allows the use of visual material that originates from distant times or places, which makes it an ideal medium in the teaching of historical, geographical and social programmes of learning.

Apart from children's own personal stories, one worthwhile way of using this technique is to record older visitors talking about their memories of childhood. Ask them to lend you as many photographs and artefacts as they can. Scan or photograph them and return them as quickly as possible because they will be precious. Children can edit the recordings and search for additional material on the internet. Invite the visitors back to see the children's work when finished.

Puppetry is the most flexible film technique for primary schools, and many of the principles of this technique apply to any type of film-making. Puppetry has many of the advantages of both animation and live action. An original fantasy world can be created, as in animation, but footage in puppet films is much less time-consuming to create: making a simple card stick puppet film can be done in five to ten hours of class time. This is important if you have a substantial story to tell. Puppet-based film-making can be a group activity that runs alongside others, or as part of a carousel of activities. For these reasons, it is puppet-based film-making that I describe in the five phases below. Each phase can be as little as an hour, or as long as you like: it really all depends on the educational focus you decide for the project.

Phase 1: Scripts and storyboards

It is worth hunting out a film script to look at on the internet – they *are* slightly different in content and layout from play scripts. They can often have long sections of narrative between spoken lines. With primary-aged children, traditional stories can be an excellent basis for films as they have a clear narrative structure, which can be readily adapted and usually have strong characters that lend themselves to puppetry. Narrative poems, too, make really good subjects for film. To make a film from a poem will require some of the liveliest textual analysis you and your children will ever do! On a more practical note: most narrative poems are divided into verses, which makes it really easy to allocate sections to groups and lines within groups.

Storyboards are useful in order to help children visualise the characters, settings and shots. Given free rein, most children produce a storyboard as a series of long shots, so it is helpful to have done some class work here beforehand. One of my favourite scenarios for storyboarding practice with a class is the following:

> Three friends are walking into town. The road takes them over a bridge and while crossing it they hear some strange sounds. They look at each other, walk to the parapet and look over. They see an acquaintance of theirs washing his cat. A conversation ensues ...

I might start by asking: Will the opening shot be from behind, in front or in profile or maybe just their feet? Perhaps we will only see the road and the friends will come into view? Will the camera follow them or will they walk past or into the frame? What angle will we see them from: above or below? How much of their bodies will we see?

Once children have cottoned on to this way of thinking, their huge experience of moving-image texts will give them plenty of ideas. To complete the exercise, they can work in groups on large sheets of paper; or individuals can be given smaller pieces to be assembled onto a large sheet. As a plenary, the groups then compare their different interpretations of the same narrative. This is a really worthwhile activity on its own for thinking about passages of written text. There is no need for the children to be able to draw well to make effective storyboards and they should certainly avoid colouring them! Arrows to indicate movement within the frame are useful. Different coloured arrows can be used for camera movements. Careful examination of storyboards will help the planning for the making of scenery and puppets. Nick Park's storyboards for some of the Wallace and Gromit movies are available in hardback (Penguin Character Books 1998). They repay close study. You might even let children see them.

Phase 2: Recording and editing sound

It is better to record the soundtrack as early in the process as possible. The aim is to provide the underlying structure and timings for your filming and editing. Audacity, the open-source, free sound recording software, is so good you really need look no further. As with all software, teacher time spent playing with the programme will repay you in time saved later on. One of the big advantages of using a separately recorded soundtrack is that you can give as many verbal directions as you like while the scene is being filmed, and children working on other activities in the background can make as much noise as they need to, because both can simply be edited out. Further, having a pre-recorded soundtrack greatly simplifies the editing of the pictorial elements.

Make sure that the children who are performing have their script in advance of the recording session and encourage them to practise reading aloud to each other. Emphasise: slow, loud and clear. The biggest problem with sound recording is achieving the quiet needed. The best answer I've found is as follows (see also Figure 9.1).

Arrange a semicircle of chairs around a microphone on a stand with a boom near the front of the room. About four seats usually works. Set the microphone on its stand so that the boom will swing around the semicircle of seats a foot or so away from the speaker's mouths. Set the microphone itself to an upright position rather than pointing at the children: this avoids 'popping' and volume surges. Plug the microphone into a laptop and the laptop into a projector. Seat the children as an audience where they can see the performers and the projected waveforms that Audacity creates while a recording is being made. Most children are respectful when others are performing and are interested in watching the waveforms that correspond to the sound they are hearing. They are also well placed for recording any special effects demanded by the script. Once the main recording is over, you can discuss the editing process while you edit. Remember to save the recording before you do any editing – just in case. It is also useful to record some silence to add in as pauses – the difference

Figure 9.1   Recording sound in the classroom

between recorded 'silence' and the artificially produced variety is amazing. It is useful to have some ambient background sounds already saved – traffic, birdsong, wind, sea, etc. This will add enormously to the atmosphere of your soundtrack. You may also wish to find or record some sound effects. The common, but not ubiquitous, sound formats wav. and MP3 will work with Audacity. Choose your music carefully. Instrumental music is best with narrative. New age and ambient music are usefully unobtrusive; folk, period or world music works well with traditional or historical tales.

Phase 3: Making puppets and scenery

Cereal packets are perfect for this purpose – stiff enough, easy to cut, and free. Show your children how to flat pack cereal boxes and they (and you) can store and transport a decent number quite easily. Encourage the children to make the puppets as large as they can fit on the box. Remind the children that the figures may well be seen in close-up, so really careful cutting and colouring is important. Any long, thin stick is fine but bamboo barbecue skewers are especially good (and remember to snip the points off!). Attach the stick with Blu-Tack rather than tape as this allows the stick to be re-attached from a different direction if the shot demands it. Sticks can be painted to match the scenery or camouflaged with a khaki colour. The aim is to keep them out of the shot, though I personally think it doesn't matter if the odd length of skewer has a moment of stardom. The puppets do not need to be jointed unless you are planning to make shadow-graph films, which is a rather more complex task. Interest is created through the use of different camera shots, rather than by puppet movement.

If you have more time, special effects puppets are fun to create. We once made a top hat for Lazy Jack that was a double layer of card separated with rolls of Blu-Tack. We framed the bottom of his hat, face and shoulders with the camera. Someone squirted yellow squeezy paint into the open top of his hat and we filmed while the 'butter' under his hat melted in the sun – and ran down over his face and shoulders.

Scenery can be made with rolls of paper or sticking two or more sheets together (landscape). Two sheets of sugar paper really is the minimum, otherwise there is no room for the camera to pan without running out of scenery. I've had children painting a Victorian street scene in sepia ink on a piece of brown counter roll the length of the classroom! Try to make sure the puppets contrast strongly with the scenery. You might use a restricted palette, dark tones or pastels for the background and contrasting colours for the puppets. Silhouettes can look really good.

Phase 4: Filming

Whether you choose to have the scenery on a vertical or horizontal surface is a matter of preference. If you are using a tripod, it's best to pin or staple the scenery to a display board and seat the puppeteers on a PE bench (see Figure 9.2). If you choose a horizontal surface, the camera will almost certainly have to be handheld (as in Figure 9.3) unless you are lucky enough to have some kind of rostrum arrangement.

Digi Blue cameras can be clipped into boom microphone stands and angled vertically down. Make sure your lighting is as good as you can

Figure 9.2   Filming on a vertical surface

Figure 9.3   Filming on a horizontal surface

get it: co-opt Anglepoise lamps, table lamps and sunlight. Reflecting both lamps and sunlight using white card will create a much more even light with less shadows for your subject. Some of the sharpest, most colourful puppet footage I ever shot was with a handheld compact camera. The scenery was flat on some tables directly under a north-facing window on a bright day. If children are doing the filming, put the scenery on the floor with the puppeteers kneeling or lying. A good bright torch is useful to create dramatic lighting effects. Plenty of rehearsal before you begin filming will save huge amounts of editing time.

Phase 5: Editing

I find editing the most absorbing part of the whole project and, given a few basic skills, there are many children who would agree with me. Editing requires so many judgements: How long should this clip be? Which is the best version? Should I use two different shots here? Should I cut or fade? Which needs more weight: the sound or the video? It is like sculpture, helping the meaning emerge from the mass of material.

However, there will always be children (and teachers) who don't enjoy this process. If speed is of the essence, editing may simply consist of putting all the clips end to end and, if they have been carefully planned and executed, this may allow for a reasonable result. For really fast viewing – for Drama or PE feedback, say – drop your clips into a folder in the My Videos folder, check they are in the right order and press Play All.

Editing is not really a spectator sport. Depending on the age and experience of the children, this may mean the whole class being involved in doing a quick rough edit on the interactive whiteboard (and tidying it up yourself after school), and/or dividing the sound and video footage into chunks for small groups to edit and save as mini movies which you or your resident geek can stitch together later. Children usually love special effects and transitions and sprinkle them around their movies like sugar. Insist that if they want to use any transition other than a cut or a fade, it must serve a purpose, i.e. it must enhance or support the meaning. Giving 'it looks nice' as a reason for using it simply will not do.

One of the great advantages of editing video to fit a soundtrack is that the soundtrack usually makes it clear what is needed visually. A good, crisp narrative makes it much easier to choose which clip, which bit and how much to use.

Publishing your film

One of the joys of film-making is the opportunity it offers for collaboration. Viewing film can also be a shared experience, both with whole classes watching and discussing films together and as viewers sharing their thoughts online. I love seeing people's online comments on 'my' films and I have no reason to suppose children feel differently.

The single biggest issue with putting video online is that of child protection. Most schools now issue a contract at the beginning of each year for parents to sign, giving their permission for video of their children to be displayed online. However, with live action video featuring individual children, it is still probably in the school's best interests to seek specific permission. The time and effort required to do this is a strong reason for using mainly animation and puppetry or masks in the primary school.

In a rehearsed piece, it is relatively simple to avoid showing children whose parents want them excluded, but more difficult where filming occurs during normal classroom activities. A simple way of avoiding showing 'excluded' children is to ask them to wear a large sticky label. This means they are easier for the camera operator or editor to spot.

So is it possible to find a safe place to publish video? The school learning platform or virtual learning environment (VLE) would seem to offer the best answer, though not all providers currently offer very good video display facilities. Most online video hosts provide a code snippet which can be pasted into the learning platform so that the video can be viewed there. However, in most, though not all, cases the video can still be viewed on the host site. Some hosts will make your videos invisible on their site – for a fee. Alternatively, there are a growing number of video-hosting services designed with education in mind which check and filter the videos on their sites.

The second big issue is copyright law. Downloading material from online sources to use for educational purposes is legal, but re-publishing that material as if it were your own work or for commercial gain is not. For example, in one of the Media Studies courses I teach, children cut up and use videos from YouTube to create their own film trailers, but I will not publish these to our Learning Platform or beyond.

Conclusion

The ability to sub-divide and categorise is necessary for a precise, analytic understanding of the world. The ability to synthesise – to use knowledge and building blocks for new ideas – is of equal importance, but is often less well served by our education system. As a result, many learners feel that school learning is incoherent and they become alienated from learning communities. An over-emphasis on analytical approaches can mean that learners are not encouraged to think in creative, original ways, nor to feel that independent thinking has anything much to do with learning.

By taking a bicycle saddle and handlebars and representing them as a bull's head, Picasso offered us a new way of seeing both bicycle and bull, and also a deeper understanding of our own perceptions. The film-making process likewise pulls together a wide range of competences from the curriculum and beyond. By applying them in this new context, we strengthen and deepen the network of skills, knowledge and understanding that we need in order to make meanings. To put it another way, film-making can be the 'digital glue' that holds this network together.

Reference

Park, N. (1998) *Wallace and Gromit: The Wrong Trousers – Storyboard Collection* (ed. B. Sibley.) London: BBC Worldwide/Penguin Character Books.

📁 Case Study 2

Peterborough's Film Experience

Janet MacPhee

Peterborough decided several years ago to capitalise on the appetite children have for watching films by exploiting the contribution film education could make to learning. The decision to focus time and resources for this was made in order to support children's writing in a way that would motivate and inspire them.

Three opportunities were planned to raise the profile of film and the use of film-related activities in classrooms across the city. Four Peterborough teachers took part in the BFI 'lead practitioners' training for moving-image media literacy. The expertise and enthusiasm the teachers gained from the training was channelled into lesson units for their own schools; they also led workshops for teaching colleagues in the city. At the same time, a three-year boys' writing project for 11 schools began, using film as the prime motivator. The third opportunity encouraged children to use their growing knowledge and understanding of films to make their own. These films were then entered into an OSCARS-style film award event organised by the local authority. This showcased children's films on a cinema-size screen in front of an audience of over 1000 people.

Monitoring and evaluation of the film activities showed many things, some expected, some not. It was hoped that the boys involved would be motivated to write to a higher standard, which is indeed what happened. Eighty per cent of the schools in the writing project reported a significant increase in the percentage of boys on target for writing. The teachers who took part in the BFI scheme reported excellent progress in boys' writing through the film-focused work they had planned. A less expected, but very welcome outcome was the motivation and desire of many teachers and teaching assistants who wanted to improve their own skills in film-making in order to support learning.

Using film in literacy lessons has been fantastic for motivating children to develop their ideas, vocabulary and general language skills in relation to writing. Taking a favourite film as a starting point and using ICT and

(Continued)

appropriate software to break down the film into manageable sections has proved to be a significant factor in improving children's writing. It has enabled all of the children, but especially the boys, to build their own writing around a focus that means something to them and in which they can become completely immersed. (Head teacher)

Making their own films has been a magical experience for many children, giving them an understanding of the technical and creative process that allows the effective expression of a story or an idea. The film awards provide a real audience and purpose for the children's efforts, one that is appreciated city-wide. The awards have gone from strength to strength, attracting local and national business and media support. They have been the main driver in encouraging interest in, and engagement with, film-making in Peterborough schools.

Index

DIGITAL LITERACIES
Social Learning and Classroom Practices

Edited by **Victoria Carrington** *University of South Australia* and **Muriel Robinson** *Bishop Grosseteste University College, Lincoln*

'This immensely readable book injects a note of passion and urgency into the ongoing discourse on the place of digital literacies in the school curriculum'
- *British Journal of Educational Technology*

Facebook, blogs, texts, computer games, instant messages The ways in which we make meanings and engage with each other are changing. Are you a student teacher trying to get to grips with these new digital technologies? Would you like to find ways to make use of them in your classroom?

Digital technologies are an everyday part of life for students and Understanding Digital Literacies explores the ways in which they can be used in schools. Carrington and Robinson provide an insight into the research on digital technologies, stressing its relevance for schools, and suggest ways to develop new, more relevant pedagogies, particularly for social learning, literacy and literate practices. With a practical focus, the examples and issues explored in this book will help you to analyse your own practice and to carry out your own small-scale research projects.

Explaining the theoretical issues and demonstrating their practical implementation, this topical book will be an essential resource to new student teachers on undergraduate and PGCE courses, and those returning to postgraduate study.

ABRIDGED CONTENTS
PART A - DIGITAL TEXTS IN AND OUT OF SCHOOL \ PART B - CHANGING LITERACIES \ PART C - CHANGING LITERACIES, CHANGING PEDAGOGIES \ PART D - INTERCONNECTIVITY

PUBLISHED IN ASSOCIATION WITH THE UKLA
2009 • 184 pages
Cloth (978-1-84787-037-7) / Paper (978-1-84787-038-4)

ALSO FROM SAGE

MEDIA LITERACY IN SCHOOLS
Practice, Production and Progression

Andrew Burn *Institute of Education, The London Knowledge Lab* and **James Durran** *Parkside Community College, Cambridge*

Includes CD-Rom

'Intriguing and timely...I whole heartedly recommend this text to teacher educators and their trainees, certainly across English and the Arts, but arguably to all engaged in considering critical pedagogy across the curriculum' - *ESCalate*

A range of case studies are presented which show how digital media work, from video editing to computer game authoring, can be developed in schools, drawing on children's own cultural knowledge. It also shows the benefits of such projects in terms of learning outcomes and increased self-esteem for a range of learners. The book comes with a CD-Rom of children's work from the various case study projects, exhibiting the high standard of moving image work, animations and computer games that can be produced with the help of this text.

With an integrated approach drawing together practice, theory and research, the book will help teachers to plan for and develop their own media projects in school. It offers advice on integrating media work across the curriculum (in English and media classes as well as in ICT and citizenship), and presents a model of progression which shows how learning can develop from the first years of secondary school through to GCSE level. In line with current government initiatives to open up curriculum boundaries, the book shows how to plan for longer periods of time for these projects.

CONTENTS

1. What Is Media Literacy? \ 2. Designing Superheroes: Cultural Functions of Comic Strip Literacy \ 3. Animation, Moving Image Literacy and Creativity \ 4. Hospital Dramas: Critical Creativity and Moving Image Literacy \ 5. Teaching Horror: Interpretation as Digital Anatomy \ 6. Selling Chocolate: Rhetoric, Representation and Agency \ 7. Game Literacy: Ludic and Narrative Design \ 8. The Horizontal Angle: Media Literacy Accross the Curriculum \ 9. The Vertical Angle: Progression in Media Literacy \ 10. Back to the Future: Possibilities and Pitfalls for Media Literacy

2007 • 208 pages

Cloth (978-1-4129-2215-9) / Paper (978-1-4129-2216-6) / Electronic (978-1-84860-474-2)

ALSO FROM SAGE